Praise for *The 12 Powers of a Marketing Leader*

"Align your customer's needs with your company's process and you'll find yourself creating or leading a market sector. *The 12 Powers of a Marketing Leader* shows you how! Barta and Barwise have conducted critical primary research to produce an astounding new framework that will change the way you market your company and meet your customers' needs! The framework, derived from comprehensive new research, offers everything you need to know to be a superior market leader! Thank you, Barta and Barwise, for sharing your secrets to success!"

—Marshall Goldsmith, The Thinkers 50
#1 Leadership Thinker in the World

"This is the book we've all been waiting for. A masterful dissection of what it really takes to lead marketing, written in a pragmatic, compelling way that everyone can use to grow their business and further their career. In a world where the fundamentals of marketing are being challenged daily by technology, it provides a roadmap for how to lead, despite the rapidly changing context. The 12 principles identify what really matters—with insight and wisdom."

—Syl Saller, Global CMO, Diageo,
Marketing Society Leader of the Year 2015

"A must-read for every present and future CMO who cares about making a difference."

—Seth Godin, author of *All Marketers Are Liars*

"Barta and Barwise show in this thoughtful book how, by realigning their role, marketers can contribute significantly more both to their companies' success and to their own career paths. Research-based, but brought to life by human beings."

—Sir Martin Sorrell, founder and CEO, WPP

"A persuasive and well-researched perspective on the opportunities open to marketers to lead for change, both inside their organizations and outside. Important reading for anyone wishing to flourish in this most exciting and dynamic field of corporate life."

—Paul Polman, CEO, Unilever

"Stuffed full of sound analysis, crucial career advice, and fascinating case studies—this is an effortless must-read for the ambitious marketer."

—Gavin Patterson, CEO, BT

"A truly insightful guide to how good marketing executives can become outstanding leaders and enhance the value of marketing within their organizations."
—Joan Kaloustian, managing director Corporate Marketing,
MUFG Union Bank

"Here is a must-read book for marketers as leaders. If you have a cause to promote, an ambition to lead, and a desire to perform on the main stage, not in the studio, pursue the practical guidance in these pages and a permanent seat at the top table, if not at its head, will be yours."
—Richard Hytner, author, *Consiglieri: Leading from the Shadows,*
founder, beta baboon, former DY Chairman, Saatchi & Saatchi Worldwide

"Barta and Barwise lay out a clear and compelling roadmap for helping marketing practitioners become high-impact enterprise leaders. Their success model is deeply grounded in data and experience and provides a framework that works within the ever-changing world of modern marketing."
—Peter Horst, CMO, The Hershey Company

"This book rejects the 'one leader fits anywhere' mentality, and makes a powerful case that leadership practices are ideally tailored to a specific functional area—such as marketing. By meshing relevant research along with personal experience, the authors also make a compelling and incisive argument that leading a group of marketing professionals differs dramatically from being a consummate practitioner."
—Jack Zenger, CEO of Zenger Folkman and
bestselling coauthor of *The Extraordinary Leader*

"The first evidence-based toolset to 'lead marketing.' A must-read for anyone who is serious about leading—not just doing—marketing."
—Bernie Jaworski, Drucker Chair in Management
and the Liberal Arts, Drucker School of Management

"Great marketing leadership is a vital part of driving business growth. This book gets under the skin of what makes a great marketing leader with vital, practical lessons which can be applied to help anyone focus toward future career success."
—Peter Markey, CMO, Post Office

"The world needed a book that could show the power of combining leadership and marketing skills. This might just become the bible for marketing leaders."
—Sherilyn Shackell, founder & CEO of The Marketing Academy

THE
12 POWERS OF
A MARKETING
LEADER

How to Succeed by Building
Customer *and* Company Value

THOMAS BARTA
PATRICK BARWISE

New York   Chicago   San Francisco   Athens   London
Madrid   Mexico City   Milan   New Delhi
Singapore   Sydney   Toronto

2 3 4 5 6 7 8 9   LCR   21 20 19 18 17

ISBN   978-1-259-83471-4
MHID   1-259-83471-9

e-ISBN   978-1-259-83472-1
e-MHID   1-259-83472-7

This publication is designed to provide accurate and authoritative information in regard to the subject matter covered. It is sold with the understanding that neither the author nor the publisher is engaged in rendering legal, accounting, securities trading, or other professional services. If legal advice or other expert assistance is required, the services of a competent professional person should be sought.

—From a Declaration of Principles Jointly Adopted by a Committee of the American Bar Association and a Committee of Publishers and Associations

Library of Congress Cataloging-in-Publication Data
Names: Barta, Thomas, author. | Barwise, Patrick, author.
Title: The 12 powers of a marketing leader : how to succeed by building
   customer and company value / by Thomas Barta and Patrick Barwise.
Other titles: Twelve powers of a marketing leader
Description: 1 Edition. | New York : McGraw-Hill Education, 2016.
Identifiers: LCCN 2016012343 (print) | LCCN 2016033056 (ebook) | ISBN
   9781259834714 (hardback : alk. paper) | ISBN 1259834719 (alk. paper) |
   ISBN 1259834727 ()
Subjects: LCSH: Marketing. | Customer relations. | Leadership. | BISAC:
   BUSINESS & ECONOMICS / Marketing / General.
Classification: LCC HF5415 .B3597 2016 (print) | LCC HF5415 (ebook) | DDC
   658.8--dc23
LC record available at https://na01.safelinks.protection.outlook.com/?url=https% 3a%2f%2flccn.
loc.gov%2f2016012343&data=01%7c01%7ccheryl.ringer%40mheducation.com%7c52e6128e92
da4f36eeb008d3b16c5cb1%7cf919b1efc0c347358fca0928ec39d8d5%7c0&sdata=1tRFfH7agfU
pyg053CR05OQxHoQO4%2bVJi94rbQinqcc%3d

To our families.

CONTENTS

Authors' Note   vii
Introduction: *Doing* Marketing Isn't the Same as *Leading* Marketing   1

SECTION I   Mobilize Your Boss
Power #1   Tackle Only Big Issues   17
Power #2   Deliver Returns, No Matter What   41
Power #3   Work Only with the Best   57

SECTION II   Mobilize Your Colleagues
Power #4   Hit the Head and the Heart   65
Power #5   Walk the Halls   73
Power #6   You Go First   85

SECTION III   Mobilize Your Team
Power #7   Get the Mix Right   95
Power #8   Cover Them in Trust   115
Power #9   Let the Outcomes Speak   131

SECTION IV   Mobilize Yourself
Power #10   Fall in Love with Your World   149
Power #11   Know How You Inspire   169
Power #12   Aim Higher   183

It's Time for Your Launch   191
Appendix: About the Research   195
Sources   207
Acknowledgments   215
Index   219

AUTHORS' NOTE

This is a leadership book to help you, as a marketer, create more value for your company and greater career success for yourself.

The lessons you'll find here are based on the largest global study ever conducted on marketing leadership.

INTRODUCTION
| | | |

Doing Marketing Isn't the Same as *Leading* Marketing

You are a marketer.

You have a passion for brands. You understand the market. You are your company's linchpin for customer focus.

For years, CEOs have wanted companies to be more market oriented and innovative. Today, digital technology offers even more opportunities—and more pressure—to serve customers better.

In principle, your spot in the organization should be exalted. Your perspectives as a marketer should be in high demand. Top management should respect and look to you as it makes key decisions.

Unfortunately, things don't always work that way.

Despite endlessly saying they want to be more customer focused, many firms don't have a marketer in the top team. Too few CMOs make it to CEO, and marketers' reputation with CEOs is mixed (as we'll show). At the writing of this book, the domain Influentialmarketers.com was still available. It's symptomatic.

Many marketers are great at *doing* marketing. They excel at things like customer understanding, brand communications, and social media campaigns.

Nonetheless, many wish they had more traction inside their own companies. They work hard to help their company grow, but their efforts aren't always translating into internal influence and stellar careers.

Our research, which we will describe momentarily, bears this out.

Seventy-one percent of marketers believed their business impact was high, but just 44 percent were satisfied with their career path. The marketers' bosses took an even bleaker view: of all their direct reports, the bosses put marketers *last* in career success.

Failure as a marketer is a big issue—not just for you but for your company, too. If you fail in making your organization customer focused, its long-term profits will suffer. And if you move on, you'll perhaps take years of customer understanding, new product ideas, and growth strategies with you.

CEOs and marketers have an obligation, then, to be jointly successful. But how?

The solution lies with you, the marketer: up until now, you've probably been putting most of your eggs in the marketing skills basket. That is, you know how to do things like position the brand and create promotions that customers love.

And we salute you for being expert in those things. They've gotten you far. But as we'll show you: they're not enough to maximize your business impact and career success.

Alongside your expertise in marketing skills, you must also become expert in marketing leadership. It's a very different basket. What's in it?

Leading marketing isn't just about serving the customer. It's also about increasing and using your knowledge and marketing's influence inside the organization to improve the end-to-end customer experience. It's about mobilizing your boss, your colleagues, your team, and yourself to maximize the overlap between customers' needs and the company's needs. That, then, is what this book will teach you.

This isn't a marketing book. It's a leadership book for marketers.

You have an important choice to make: you can choose to continue as just a technical marketer. Thanks to digital, you shouldn't get bored—there will always be interesting new things happening. But you're unlikely to create significant impact for the company. You may even end up frustrated by your limited career success.

This book offers you a more ambitious alternative—almost certainly better for both the company and yourself. Use your leadership ability—and the new digital opportunities—to achieve what few firms do really well: connect customers and the company.

The Three Truths

This book is based on a comprehensive study of chief marketing officers* (discussed in more detail in the Appendix). The study can be divided into three parts.

In the first part, the answers came from top marketers themselves. 1,232 senior marketers took an extensive self-assessment, so we could understand what they know, how they lead, and how successful they consider themselves in terms of both their impact on business performance and their personal career success.

In the second part, we looked at CMOs through the eyes of others. We analyzed 67,278 360-degree assessment responses from superiors, coworkers, and direct reports who rated marketers along with leaders from other disciplines such as finance and sales.†

In the third part, we developed insights from interviews with over 100 CMOs, CEOs, and leadership experts about what matters for success as a senior marketing leader.

---

* As job titles in marketing vary widely, we are using the terms *chief marketing officer,* *senior marketer,* and *senior marketing leader* interchangeably to describe those in charge of marketing.
† The sample comprised 7,429 marketing and nonmarketing leaders.

What we found has completely changed our view on what it takes for a marketer to "make it."

Our research has also given us hope: as a marketer, you *can* succeed by systematically applying a number of leadership skills that are particular to marketing.

Let's take a look at the research results. We'll begin with three insights, which we call "the three truths."

Truth #1: Your power lies in the space where customer and company needs overlap (the "V-Zone").

Our research confirms that marketing success is about maximizing the overlap between customer and company needs. We call this overlap the "Value Creation Zone" . . . or "V-Zone," for short. Creating that match, however, isn't what marketers do naturally.

To understand what's inside the V-Zone, let's first look at what's outside of it.

Suppose you spend most of your time acquiring new customers. Bringing in customers from the competition, or customers who are new to the market, is what marketers do, right? For you, acquiring customers is your business's lifeblood.

Figure I.1 The V-Zone

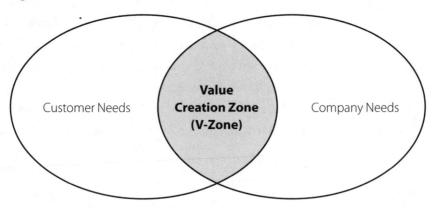

Nonetheless, the CEO doesn't share your view. In top management's opinion, acquiring new customers—at least the way you're currently doing it—is expensive and wasteful because so many of them leave before the company has gotten its money back.

Instead of putting so much effort into customer acquisition, the top team's priority is to increase customer retention. They feel the business would profit more if the customers they already had enjoyed a better experience, stayed longer, spent more money with the company, and recommended it to others.

That kind of disconnect between marketing and the top team would spell trouble. You'd be working outside the V-Zone, because what you (and some customers) care about most and what the CEO cares about most don't match. In that example, the company and most customers would suffer, and so would your career.

So what's it like working inside the V-Zone?

When marketers work there, they create value for customers (products, services, and experiences that meet their needs), value for the company (revenue and profit), and value for themselves (greater influence and better careers).

Finding the overlap between customer needs and company needs is the principle behind successful marketing leadership.

As a marketing leader, your natural focus is on customers (*doing* marketing). But in every organization, people from different departments need to work together in creating the customer experience. It seems only logical, then, that, to succeed, an exclusive focus on customers isn't enough. To get things done for customers, marketers must also understand how to serve the needs of the organization, too. Often times, these needs don't overlap easily and there will be tension. Marketing leadership is about trying to increase that overlap of customer needs *and* company needs.

Our research shows that the most successful marketing leaders are indeed those who maximize the overlap between customer needs and company needs (the V-Zone).

Truth #2: Success in marketing is about mastering "The 12 Powers of a Marketing Leader."
In our research, we found 12 important sets of leadership behaviors that determine success as a marketing leader. We call these behaviors "the 12 Powers."

For the marketers in our study, how they lead was the number one driver of their business impact and career success. Functional marketing skills, of course, matter too. As a marketer, to succeed, you still have to *do* marketing. But these technical skills, for long-term success, are just your ticket of entry.

To create long-term value by increasing the overlap between customer needs and company needs, marketing leadership skills are paramount.

The 12 Powers themselves fall into four bigger groups: mobilizing your *boss*, mobilizing your *colleagues*, mobilizing your *team*, and mobilizing *yourself.* They complement what you already do each day: mobilizing *customers*!

We calculated how much each of the 12 Powers contributed to the business impact and career success of the senior marketers in our research.

For example, for the marketers in our study, **Power #1: Tackle Only Big Issues**, accounted for 10 percent of (the explicable variation in) business impact, and the same (10 percent) for career success.*

Success as a marketing leader is about mastering and applying the leadership skills that help you maximize the V-Zone.

Sherilyn Shackell, founder and CEO of The Marketing Academy, summarized it this way: "The challenge for CMOs is that they now need people who are doing jobs that they themselves have never done—roles that probably weren't even in existence five or ten years ago. Leadership capabilities of top marketers have to be exceptional to impact companies going through so much change."

Let's take a closer look.

---

* See the Appendix for details.

Table I.1 The 12 Powers of a Marketing Leader
(Contribution of each power to the explicable variation in marketers' business impact and career success)

MOBILIZE YOUR BOSS

Power #1. Tackle Only Big Issues (Business: 10%, Career: 10%)	Make sure that what you work on is inside the V-Zone: it matters for both customers *and* the company (as judged by the CEO). And put a price tag on your work, so people see why what you're doing matters.
Power #2. Deliver Returns, No Matter What (Business: 12%, Career: 3%)	Financial returns should be your priority. Being seen as an effective investor will also help your standing at the top and, ultimately, make more resources available to you.
Power #3. Work Only with the Best (Business: 1%, Career: 2%)	Mobilizing your boss is easier if you work with the best external people who will deliver great work. (This is the weakest of the 12 Powers but helpful at the margin).

MOBILIZE YOUR COLLEAGUES

Power #4. Hit the Head and the Heart (Business: 3%, Career: 7%)	You can't mobilize colleagues if they don't listen to you. Tell them a real-life story that offers hope; get into their hearts as well as their heads.
Power #5. Walk the Halls (Business: 13%, Career: 13%)	As a marketer, you won't change the world by sitting at your desk. You have to go out and engage people to make things happen. This is one of the most important of the 12 Powers.
Power #6. You Go First (Business: 6%, Career: 12%)	Aim to lead from the front. Be the change you want to see. Act as a role model for others.

MOBILIZE YOUR TEAM

Power #7. Get the Mix Right (Business: 20%, Career: 7%)	You need the right mix of team skills, styles, and personalities (including yours). To build a powerful tribe, align the team closely around a common goal.

Table I.1 The 12 Powers of a Marketing Leader *(continued)*

Power #8. Cover Them in Trust (Business: 4%, Career: 3%)	To enlarge the V-Zone, you must build a team where people have the trust and confidence to ask for forgiveness if things go wrong, not for permission before they do anything.
Power #9. Let the Outcomes Speak (Business: 6%, Career: 9%)	Love it or hate it: as team leader, you are also the judge. You must set the standards, weigh performance, and ensure consequences when needed.
MOBILIZE YOURSELF	
Power #10. Fall in Love with Your World (Business: 18%, Career: 9%)	This is another really important Power. As a marketing leader, you need to know your stuff (customers, products, and industry). This knowledge can also inspire you and others.
Power #11. Know How You Inspire (Business: 2%, Career: 12%)	Inspiration is a marketing leader's biggest weapon. The more you understand why and how you inspire people today, the more you can use these abilities to mobilize others.
Power #12. Aim Higher (Business: 5%, Career: 13%)	The road ahead will sometimes be bumpy. Successful marketing leaders aim high and hang on to their dream to make big things happen—even against the odds.

The leadership skills you need in order to win in marketing are very particular—the 12 Powers of a Marketing Leader.

Truth #3: You weren't born a marketing leader. You must become one.

Much to our surprise, we found that personality matters very little when it comes to a marketing leader's success. Instead, almost everyone can learn the critical marketing leadership behaviors. What may sound counterintuitive at first makes lots of sense when you take a second look.

The leadership skills needed in marketing differ significantly from those needed by leaders in other business functions. That's because marketers have to bridge three distinct gaps that are especially wide in marketing:

- *A trust gap:* Most of your work is about the future (e.g., projected revenue). So your bosses and colleagues will always, to a degree, doubt what you say.
- *A power gap:* A great customer experience involves many departments. So most of the people you need to create such an experience won't report to you directly.
- *A skills gap:* Marketing technology is changing almost monthly. So you'll never know as much as you need to know. That skills gap isn't your fault—but it's a major challenge every marketer faces.

As a marketing leader, you'll need specific leadership skills and behaviors to close these gaps:

- First, mobilize your *boss* to support your activities, even if you can't always prove the outcome (Powers #1–3).
- Second, mobilize *colleagues* who don't report to you so that, together, you can create a great customer experience (Powers #4–6).
- Third, mobilize *your team* to fight alongside you, even while they're learning all the new technical marketing skills needed for the digital age (Powers #7–9).
- Fourth, mobilize *yourself,* to keep going and inspire those around you to expand the V-Zone (Powers #10–12).

These skills and behaviors—and, therefore, marketers' business impact and career success—are not based much on personality.

In our study, we measured CMOs against the well-established "Big Five" personality traits: openness to experience, dependability/self-discipline, extraversion, agreeableness (how *nice* people are), and emotional resilience. These personality traits explained only about 3.3 percent of senior marketers' business impact and 8.7 percent of their career success.

So, yes, your personality matters a bit and, as a marketer, you're probably somewhat different from your nonmarketing peers, as we'll show you later.

But leading marketing successfully takes specific skills you couldn't possibly be born with. Personality (how you are wired) is only a secondary factor.

So, no excuses: whoever you are and whatever your personality, you can learn the skills to be successful as a marketing leader.

Why Your (and Your Company's) Success Matters to Us

We have a dual objective for this book: we want you, as a marketing leader, to have a better career (and, quite simply, more fun). But we also want your customers and companies to benefit.

After all, if you succeed in increasing the overlap between your customers' needs and your company's needs, the customers will get a better deal, your company's business performance will improve, and your career will thrive.

For these benefits to occur, you must change the game and take charge. We want to help you do this.

Here's why this work is important to us.

Even as a child, Thomas was crazy about marketing and advertising. For instance, when his family gathered around the TV to watch programs, Thomas was more excited about the commercials—which he could recite by heart. ("American Express: Don't leave home without it . . .")

It makes sense, then, that he headed into a career as a marketer—eventually becoming the leader of Kimberly-Clark's European Kleenex household marketing team. There, he experienced firsthand the joys and frustrations of marketing leadership in a complex consumer goods company that had to operate in a challenging market.

From his experience as a marketing leader, Thomas was convinced that marketers needed a stronger voice in the C-suite, so he joined McKinsey, where he became a partner—often working on strategy with CEOs from around the globe.

Thomas realized that while most CEOs were open to marketing, many struggled to understand exactly what marketers actually did and how their work helped the company. Even more, Thomas observed that many marketers didn't connect well with CEOs.

As a dean of McKinsey's internal leadership program, Thomas increasingly spent time coaching CMOs to help raise and achieve their organizational aspirations.

His passion to help CMOs succeed turned into a new career as an expert on marketing leadership and led him to leave McKinsey and launch the research program behind this book.

Patrick's theme throughout his career has been the need for organizations to become more customer focused and—in particular—how to make that happen in practice. Since joining London Business School in 1976 after an early career at IBM, he has published widely on management, marketing, and media, including his prize-winning 2004 book with Seán Meehan, *Simply Better: Winning and Keeping Customers by Delivering What Matters Most*. He also served for many years as a trustee and then chairman of Which?, the world's second-largest consumer organization, and has been involved in two successful business start-ups in the online market research space. Initially Thomas's mentor on this book project, he became so enthused by it that he asked if he could join as a coauthor—a request that Thomas was more than happy to accept.

So for both of us, this is personal! If we can help you and other marketers improve your leadership skills and impact within your companies, you, your customers, and your companies will all benefit. That's a powerful motivation for us, as well as for you.

Making It Happen

Because the purpose of business is to create a customer, the business enterprise has two—and only two—basic functions: marketing and innovation.

—Peter Drucker (1954)

Every CEO knows that the key to long-term business performance is profitably meeting customers' needs better than the competition. It's easy to say but has proved hard to put into practice.

Marketers should be in the forefront of making customer focus happen—especially in a digital world, where many CEOs are looking to them to lead the way to more customer–focused innovation and delivery.

It's a great time for marketers to change course and take things into their own hands. When we recently raised this with Marshall Goldsmith, one of the world's top leadership coaches, Marshall's response was: "Marketers must concentrate on what they can change—and that's more than they think."

Mastering the 12 Powers will help you to expand your company's V-Zone, boosting both your business impact and your long-term career success.

Don't wait to be asked. Now is the time for you to take charge and lead.

■ ■ ■

In the following twelve chapters, we'll share stories of what successful marketing leaders did, show you evidence from our research, and, most important, give you tips and ideas for how you can master each of the 12 Powers.

By the time you reach the end of this book, you'll have gone through all the 12 Powers and—we hope—developed a personal action plan to set yourself on the path toward long-term success.

Before you start, try to complete the short self-assessment quiz below (based on one of our comprehensive assessment instruments). It should take no more than five minutes to answer the questions. The results will give you, at the start of your leadership journey, a rough feel for where you stand today.

Enough said. Let's get going.

The 12 Powers of Marketing Leaders— Where Am I Today?

For each question, ask yourself how well the statement applies to you. Be as honest as possible. Write your score next to each statement:

5 – Applies completely

4 – Applies somewhat

3 – It depends

2 – Doesn't really apply

1 – Doesn't apply at all

_____ 1. In my team, I have built a high level of trust and confidence.

_____ 2. Others can see that my actions help achieve our business goals.

_____ 3. My activities create high returns for the business.

_____ 4. I always mobilize people in the organization with my vision.

_____ 5. I know myself and my impact on others.

_____ 6. I always inspire people with my customer vision or story.

_____ 7. In my team, people take accountability very seriously.

_____ 8. I have a clear vision of what I want to achieve in my life.

_____ 9. My priorities are fully aligned with those of the top team.

_____ 10. I have built a team with the right skills and a clear direction, to solve our biggest business issues.

_____ 11. I'm a true expert when it comes to my customers, products, and industry.

_____ 12. I always work with the best external people.

The 12 Powers—Your Results

Please enter your score for each statement into the table below and add them up.

Mobilize Yourself	Mobilize Your Boss
Statement 5 _____	Statement 3 _____
Statement 8 _____	Statement 9 _____
Statement 11 _____	Statement 12 _____
TOTAL _____ (of 15)	TOTAL _____ (of 15)

Mobilize Your Team	Mobilize Your Colleagues
Statement 1 _____	Statement 2 _____
Statement 7 _____	Statement 4 _____
Statement 10 _____	Statement 6 _____
TOTAL _____ (of 15)	TOTAL _____ (of 15)

How to read your scores for each of the four areas, assuming you've been neither too tough nor too lenient on yourself:

13–15:   You are already mastering these Powers of marketing leadership very well.

9–12:   You're mastering some of these Powers, but you aren't using them as much as you could.

3–8:   You aren't yet showing many of these Powers.

You can take a more complete online version of this profile-test here: www.marketingleader.org/download.

SECTION I MOBILIZE YOUR BOSS

"RECOGNIZING POWER IN ANOTHER DOES NOT DIMINISH YOUR OWN."

—JOSS WHEDON

| | | |

Tackle Only Big Issues

Your central question:

Am I working on the topics that matter most for the V-Zone?

As a marketing leader, if you want to have influence and help the company grow, be sure that, as far as possible, the only issues you tackle are big. What, though, constitutes a "big issue"?

A "big marketing issue" is a problem that matters a lot both to your customers and to your CEO and top team. Such a "big issue" always sits right inside the V-Zone. And when you're tackling big issues, your influence as a marketing leader grows.

For an example, let's look at a big issue from the career of Dee Dutta.

In the past few years, Dee has worked as CMO of top international brands that include Sony and Visa. But he laid the foundation for his distinguished global marketing career in a much smaller role in the early 1990s, as a head of consumer marketing.

At the time, Dee worked at mobile operator One2One (which later went on to become T-Mobile).

Then, buying a mobile phone wasn't for everyone, because making calls was expensive. And, since customers received a bill only at month's end, One2One was worried that they would rack up high charges and default on their payment. The company understandably avoided doing business with people who might be credit risks.

Dee, however, saw things differently. A son of immigrants, he knew firsthand what it was like to live on a tight budget. He'd even had to turn down family and friends who'd asked, "Can you get me a phone?"

Around the same time, at a company-wide meeting, Dee heard the CEO talk about how the market was slowly saturating and how the company needed new ways of securing profitable growth.

Dee was keen, then, on helping both the customer and the company. He wanted to enlarge the V-Zone.

Together with colleagues, he picked up an idea that had been floating around the company but had never been properly explored: Why not let customers pay in advance? Paying in advance would eliminate the credit risk, improve cash flow and increase revenues, while getting phones to more people. That at least was the theory.

Dee's peers weren't convinced the theory would work. The finance team was worried about the profitability, the operations group was concerned about the technical issues with prepayment, and others in the company were dubious about whether customers would want to pay for calls they hadn't yet made.

Dee, though, didn't give up. His team tackled the issues one by one and came away with a business plan and a technical solution. The first meetings with senior management went badly. People felt the plan wasn't worth the risk. Dee and his team decided to run a small-scale test.

The test results were beyond expectation. Customers were happy to pay upfront. Many of these so-called lower-income customers were actually spending more money than many existing contract customers—making the company greater profit.

Dee's team returned to the company management. This time, they had their idea, a plan, and the supporting facts. Management gave the project a green light and One2One launched the first commercially successful pay-as-you-go offer.*

The news spread fast in the world of telecoms, and pay-as-you-go is still the preferred choice for about three-quarters of global mobile users.†

Dee and his colleagues helped make a huge difference to themselves, the company, and customers around the world. All because they tackled a big issue for both customers and the company. Tackling a big issue changed everything.

Your company's survival and success depend on profitably serving customers better than competitors do. You're the linchpin of your company's customer understanding. It's your job to mobilize the organization's top leaders to serve customers better. Step one: tackle big issues.

The Issues Issue

Tackling big issues is a big success driver for marketing leaders. But too few marketers are working on the really big issues inside the V-Zone—and that's both a problem and an opportunity.

Early in our study, we spoke with international CMOs about their work, asking "What do you do?" It was interesting how different people answered. Some said things like, "I manage the brand" or "I run our marketing."

Words like these don't go down well with company leaders. In the words of marketing professor and columnist Mark Ritson, "Too many marketers go into a room full of executives from their company and

---

* A Portuguese company also gets cited as the first to bring prepay to market. It wouldn't be the first time that different people worked independently on a great idea in parallel: to name just one example, Newton and Leibnitz both invented calculus around the same time (and their Anglo-German relationship was a lot less friendly than ours).

† 2012 mobile industry revenue: 1,002 bn US$, 77% = prepaid. Source: A. T. Kearney, *The Mobile Economy*, 2013.

Contribution to Marketers' Business Impact and Career Success

Business	Tackle Only Big Issues (10%)
Career	Tackle Only Big Issues (10%)

Variation in marketing leaders' perceived business impact and career success accounted for by this power as a percentage of the total variation accounted for by all 12 Powers in the neural network model (N = 1,232). In our research, what constitutes "Tackles Only Big Issues" are behaviors like: understanding what's right for the business, aligning priorities with company leaders, thinking about the big picture, and focusing on priorities.

The Marketer's DNA-study, Barta and Barwise, 2016

warble on about the need to build brand awareness and brand equity. No one gives a [&#%], except you—and presumably you are already on board. Good marketers work out how to link what they do with what other stakeholders within the organization want—employee retention, improved profits, clearer leadership."

The best marketing leaders speak differently about their role. Our interviews with the most successful CMOs, then, had one thing in common: a top management viewpoint. Rather than talking about marketing, they spoke of the business as a whole. They didn't talk a lot about advertising, branding, or customer insights. They spoke about revenue, costs, and profit—and how they could serve the customer better. The real marketing leaders were concerned with one thing: how marketing helps the company achieve its biggest priorities.

In our study, tackling only big issues contributed 10 percent to both the marketers' business's impact and their career success.* The rest was explained by the other 11 powers—or chapters—in this book. Ten percent, though, is a lot. Our research has, for the first time, shown that focusing on big issues in the V-Zone (aligning important customer and

---

* More precisely, this factor accounted for 10 percent of the variation (in both business impact and career success) accounted for by the 12 Powers in combination. See the Appendix for details.

company needs) substantially influences marketers' business impact and career success.

In our core study, a whopping 76 percent of marketers told us they were good at finding and aligning on what matters for the business.

Unfortunately, their bosses disagreed. In the large 360-degree database we analyzed, just 46 percent of bosses believed their marketers knew where the organization was going, *and* shared this with their teams.

We weren't the only ones finding misalignment. The Economist Intelligence Unit found that 54 percent of company leaders thought their companies' marketing and business strategies weren't aligned.* The CEO of a global consumer electronics company summarized it as follows: "As a board, we worry a lot about how we can grow the franchise profitably, what our reputation is, and how to build talent. But my marketing team is more concerned with advertising and their budget. This can be pretty frustrating."

Working inside the V-Zone is key for your success. You may think you are tackling big issues—but your boss may not see it.

What's a Big V-Zone Issue?

Figuring out what the big issues are inside the V-Zone isn't always easy. Consider the following example of a large US financial institution's marketing team who worked with Thomas to strengthen their impact and contribution.

Thomas recalls: "On Day One, I asked the group to write on flipcharts the answer to a simple question, What are the main issues for your customers? The room filled with energy, and everybody wrote down their ideas quickly.

"My second question stopped the group in their tracks: What are the top three priorities of your company, as seen by the CEO—and how does your marketing work overlap with these priorities? Most participants

---

* Economist Intelligence Unit. "Outside Looking In: The CMO Struggles to Get in Sync with the C-suite," (2012).

had problems recalling what kept their boss awake at night. Fewer than half the charts showed even one overlapping item.

"My third question nearly derailed the workshop: For your top three marketing priorities, what's their value to the company? Most people dropped their pens, saying that quantifying their work is hard or even impossible."

It took a day for the team to get hold of the CEO's priorities and match them with customers' priorities (find the "big issues") and then put numbers on the resulting marketing priorities.

The new focus on big issues, however, has significantly increased the team's internal impact and reputation (and the CMO's tenure . . .).

Many marketers work hard but struggle to make what they do relevant to their bosses. The reason? They don't tackle big issues. They work outside of the V-Zone. We've all seen the symptoms: budget cuts, slow career tracks, the last place on meeting agendas, and so on.

If you work on things that don't matter to customers, you won't leave a dent in the market. If you work on things that don't matter to the CEO (or whoever leads your place), you may be "busy," but you won't be listened to internally.

As a marketing leader, aligning your agenda closely with customers *and* the company—the core of the V-Zone—is your sweet spot.

Your first priority should therefore be to find the "big issue" you can influence—an issue that tackles a top customer need and a top company need, as seen by your CEO.

One of India's top marketers, Nand Kishore Badami, CMO India & SAARC of Cisco Systems, told us: "My team and I work hard to stay on top of customer needs. But we also know the three things that keep our president and CEO awake at night. There's a customer journey and a company journey. Marketers must understand and align both."

Only when you've identified a combination of a strong customer need and a strong company need are you onto a big V-Zone issue. And to make sure people get the importance of your issue, you must give it a price tag—an estimate of how much it's worth (revenue, cost saving, profit, etc.). Even if it's only approximate, big marketing issues should always have a price tag.

Figure 1.1 Big Marketing Issues

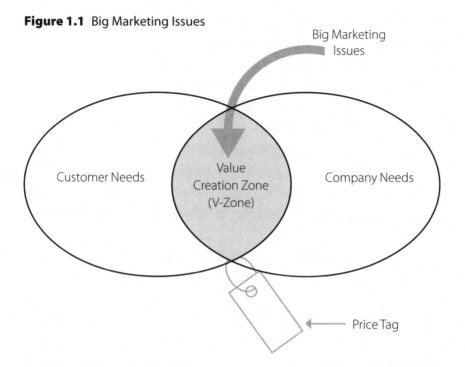

One person who knows the importance of bringing a price tag to the table is Bernhard Mattes, now CEO of Ford Germany but at one time the company's marketing manager. When Bernhard led the firm's marketing, he quickly identified a big issue: how Ford prices cars.

At the time, the hatchback and limousine versions of the Ford Mondeo, for example, had the same price. The company also included many product features in the cars, independent of whether customers wanted them or not—and charged the same price for each type of vehicle.

While all the company's marketers before him focused on marketing campaigns, Bernhard tackled a bigger, strategic issue with a large impact on the bottom line: value-based pricing. Armed with a business case (his price tag) he convinced the board to price cars based on how customers valued features, leading to lower prices for base-model cars and higher prices (and margins) for cars with extras. Many customers and the company benefited—and so did Bernhard's career.

One2One's Dee Dutta also tackled a big issue by leading with a price tag. To convince the company's management to launch pay-as-you-go offers, he and his finance colleagues drew up a detailed analysis, showing a potential annual profit of several million US dollars.

Let's take a look at how you can find the big issues inside the V-Zone—the ones customers and the CEO care about.

Find the Key Customer Needs

If you know where future growth will come from, your CEO will listen. "Marketers need to get more involved in business strategy and be able to show where markets are headed. Highlighting sources of future growth is a way of doing this," Christopher Macleod, marketing director of Transport for London, told us.

As a marketing leader, you probably already know your customers' top problems, needs, and wishes. Write them down, then cull that list into a Top 3.

Be sure your list is in the customer's language. Don't write sentences like "an engaging customer experience"—no customer speaks like that. Instead, use words your customers might use, e.g., "getting me my orders faster," "letting me purchase while I'm on the train," "washing my dark T-shirts without fading."

After making your initial list, if you're still unsure about your customers' key needs, here are additional ways of finding them (if you're already clear, skip this section):

Find "Simply Better" Customer Issues and Latent Needs

Small continuous improvements underlie the great majority of brands and businesses enjoying long-term success. The idea is simple: they focus on profitably meeting customers' basic needs "simply better" than competitors.

A good starting point, then, is in thinking about the things that are letting your customers down—the main drivers of complaints and customer dissatisfaction. Addressing these will improve your position, relative to the competition, in customers' minds.

To get further ahead of the competition, you should also look for customers' unexpressed "latent" needs. Think about ways in which you and your competitors could *all* do a better job. That will help you bring out things customers value but don't complain about not getting.

Can you find a way to be the first to serve these latent needs? You could end up raising the bar for the whole industry.

A great example of a brand that constantly delivers small continuous improvements is Colgate, which has been a leading brand for almost a century. That's quite an achievement for a product people use every day without thinking and with tough competitors such as P&G and Unilever. Colgate has continuously kept the market moving. Small innovations like MPF fluoride, Blue Minty Gel, and Colgate Total are just some examples. Few of these innovations would be seen as groundbreaking by consumers (although they invariably seem bigger to industry insiders). But they delivered relevant user benefits, to keep people buying the brand decade after decade.

Just think about the most successful companies you know: with very few exceptions, relentless incremental innovation is likely to be an important (if unglamorous) driver of their long-term success. That's even true for companies that started with a breakthrough innovation.*

There are numerous examples of what happens when brands don't focus on meeting customers' basic needs "simply better," but instead try to do too much. Fred Perry, supposedly a high-end sports fashion brand, was in a shambles when CEO John Flynn took over in 1993. Frantic efforts to grow had left it with a mishmash of high- and low-end shirts, as it tried to address more and more buyer segments. Customers were turning away, confused by the unclear positioning. Today, the brand is thriving again thanks to a streamlined collection, planned and executed with obsessive attention to detail. Most important, Fred Perry has refocused on being the preferred choice for its most loyal high-end buyers.

Everyone loves breakthrough innovations. They're extremely profitable and widely celebrated when they succeed—but they rarely do. *Incremental* (like *follower*) is almost a rude word—but, in reality, for most

---

* We know that this view is controversial and some readers may be skeptical about it. For the evidence, see Barwise and Meehan, *Simply Better*, pages 21–23 and especially *Beyond the Familiar*, pages 15–17 and 93–118.

companies, relentless incremental product and service improvements are a key driver of long-term profit growth.

Even for Apple, famous for disruptive innovation, "It was this relentless improvement that was able to beat our competitors and yield the market share that it did," said Steve Jobs at an investor conference a few months before he died. And in 2012, chief designer Sir Jonathan Ive, responsible for the design of iconic Apple products such as the iPhone and iPad, said, "Our goals are very simple—to design and make better products. If we can't make something that is better, we won't do it."

Beating the competition by being "simply better" at meeting customers' needs, week by week and year by year, is a great way to approach finding customer issues. Why? Because it forces you to find out what matters most from a customer perspective, which is often different—and more down to earth—than the company assumes.

Consider "Big Bang" Customer Issues

Another way you could think about customer needs is to create radically new ones.

Apple's famous *Think Different* theme still holds true for some well-known marketing leaders.

The most exciting and appealing customer innovation is a "big bang" transformation that takes the whole market somewhere completely new. Sometimes these big bang ideas come from customers. More often, customers don't know about or expect them. For many marketers today, "big bang" can also mean redefining what category they work in and where future value creation is likely to come from. Today, for example, most customers own their cars. In the future, they may want a mobility solution including a car on demand, a bus when it's practical, and navigation along the way.

Steve Jobs said that the iPod wouldn't exist if he'd asked customers what they wanted. A generation earlier, much the same was said about the Sony Walkman, allegedly first developed so that the company's cochairman could listen to opera on long-haul flights. Ben & Jerry's ice cream wouldn't exist if Ben Cohen hadn't tried unusually intense flavors and textured objects to please his friend Jerry Greenfield's poor taste buds. Other well-known entrepreneurs like Fred Smith (FedEx), Larry Page (Google), and Jerry Yang (Yahoo!) have all achieved big success by inventing new product categories.

Occasionally, even established corporations create what can be seen as new categories. Examples include IBM with its all-compatible System/360 mainframes and peripherals in 1964 and, on a smaller scale, P&G with its Swiffer cleaning system in 1999.

The world needs marketing leaders who come up with a breakthrough, game-changing vision, or a radical new way to meet customers' fundamental needs in a much better way than does existing solutions.

Which customer needs could you tackle? How or where people eat? Sleep? Work?

If you can find a profitable big bang vision: great. If not, no problem: the great majority of successful innovation is based on products, services, and business systems that are "simply better."

Find the Key Company Needs, as Seen by the CEO

Getting behind the company needs isn't always easy and it involves an important decision: "make or buy."

You could simply ask about company leaders' priorities and adopt them as your own (*buy*). But perhaps you believe your company leaders aren't aware of the key customer issues and it's your role to put these on the agenda (*make*). Both are reasonable strategies.

Not every marketing leader may be able to (or should) reshape the entire C-suite agenda. It's OK to go with the company's existing top priorities, provided these priorities will serve customers well and therefore are inside the V-Zone. That said: it's your judgment call. In any case it's *always* important to understand what's on the minds of your company's most senior leaders.

Getting in sync with senior leaders takes effort. Different members of the top team may have very different views about the big issues (in which case, eliciting these differences could be really valuable—if scary). But understanding the key company issues is an important investment that you should undertake.

Perhaps one lunch with your CEO will get you the full view of the top company issues. But it may not. In fact, we suggest you talk to several senior leaders to find what keeps them awake at night.

If you've been around a while, these talks should help you confirm what you know. If you are new, short meetings with company leaders will also be a powerful way to introduce yourself. By the way, you don't have to be the CMO to go out and ask: "What are the big company needs?" That's a legitimate question even for a marketing trainee. Here are some meeting tips:

1. **Go in with both an open mind and a point of view.** Don't just say "Hi, I want to find out what the big business issues are." People may think you're clueless. Instead, come in with a point of view, presenting it as an initial hypothesis. Show you're there to learn.
2. **Make the meeting important.** At the meeting itself, show a sense of urgency. You've come to discuss the important issues, and you're keen to help.
3. **Summarize the big company issues.** At the end, recap what you understand the person you're meeting thinks are the top two or three company issues, so they can confirm or correct your understanding.
4. **Think about how you could create an alliance with this leader.** Once you know which issue to tackle, alliances become key. You'll almost certainly need their support, so think about how you could help each other.

Here's an example of a meeting summary:

> **Aligning with Hannah, CFO**
>
> The burning issues
>
> 1. Remain the market leader in Latin America
> 2. Improve profitability throughout the United States
> 3. Attract and retain talent, especially in Asia
>
> First ideas for how we could align
>
> 1. Increasing the customer preference for our Lat Am products. One "lighthouse" project with fast success
> 2. Taking out costly product features few US customers use
> 3. Setting up a "best marketing team in the industry" talent project (Asia Marketing University)

People often ask us: How can I decide which big issue to tackle inside the V-Zone if I have several promising options after speaking with senior leaders? There's no silver-bullet answer to that question, but here are some criteria you can use:

1. **Biggest win–win for customers and the company.** Tackle an issue whose solution will benefit both customers and the company most. Why? Because tackling these issues will help you increase the V-Zone!
2. **Realism.** Pick an issue that appears solvable with a realistic effort.
3. **Energy.** Test your ideas with a few people. You'll soon see which ones generate the most energy. That could be the difference between failure and success.
4. **Time to success.** Pick something where you can achieve measurable progress while you're still around.

Give Your Big Issues a Price Tag (Use Powerful Data to Prove It)

"In God we trust. All others must bring data." Ed Deming's (possibly apocryphal) quote couldn't be truer for marketing leaders.

Why are CFOs so powerful? Partly because they have credible data on crucial issues for the company—costs, revenues, and profits—issues important to the CEO.

But aren't customers crucial, too? In the long term, customer data are just as important to the CEO as financial data. It's your job to find these data points for your big issue and then share them.

Most marketing data (e.g., "brand perception" or "gross rating points") isn't that interesting to CEOs. These terms—if not used in the right context—are simply too far removed from the bottom line.

Find metrics important enough that the CEO wants to see them. Use these metrics to prove your big issue and set up a regular report to monitor them. We can't underline enough how important regular reporting is for your internal standing and influence.

Just imagine the following situation: You are the brand manager of an insurance company. Customers believe your company isn't advising them well, and in surveys rate your brand poorly. Much of what customers experience is driven by the interactions with your sales team. But the sales team's activities are largely driven by short-term commissions—and sales doesn't report to you anyway. What can you do?

You could, of course, send ideas and training manuals to the sales team, hoping they'll use them. Good luck with that.

But what if, instead, you track customers' experiences and their impact on brand perception and subsequent sales? And then suggest that the sales team should be partly incentivized on customer satisfaction, which drives reputation and long-term sales? Perhaps people won't like your idea at first and may even challenge the validity of your big-issue data. But if your numbers are solid, you may soon find that your head of sales will start trying to improve what customers say about the sales team.

Nobody can ignore good data for long, especially if it is widely shared at the top of the organization and connects what customers think of your company and how much they buy as a result.

The most important people determining the customer experience probably don't report to you. But consistently showing the right big-issue data can help you, as a marketing leader, mobilize people much better than any command-and-control reporting line can.

In the process of writing this book, we spoke to a number of marketing leaders about the power of numbers to help expand the V-Zone. While they all agreed on the importance of data, some mentioned important real-life constraints: What if urgent decisions don't allow time to collect data? What if we can't afford proper research to prove our points? What if we have great data but our CEO still trusts his gut more?

There are no magic answers to these questions: marketing is always the art of the possible. But don't use them as an excuse to rely on seat-of-the-pants decision making. Start gathering data, test some ideas, try what works, and—over time—develop your best evidence-based approach to the big issue in your company. Here are some tips for how to go about proving your big V-Zone issue with data:

1. **Give your big V-Zone issue an absolute number (a price tag).**
   No matter which issue you pick, provide an estimate of how much it is worth, ideally in money terms. If your big issue is, for example, to retain an additional two percent of customers per annum, how much could this be worth? If you want to get more of the older customers in your market, what's the annual revenue or profit potential? Some of these estimates will be hard to calculate. Work with your finance team or other experts to at least get a ballpark number.

2. **In reporting, wherever possible, link customer issues with company issues.** For instance, the CMO of a retailer shows how customer satisfaction (a customer issue) drives share of wallet (how much people spend with that retailer as a percentage of their total expenditure in its market, a company issue). The head of marketing

for a bank tracks customer transactions (a company issue) and links them to brand preference (a customer issue). The sales and marketing manager of a midsize industrial services firm shows how customer advocacy (how likely customers are to recommend others to buy or not to buy from the company) drives long-term sales (a company issue).

3. **Keep reporting (very) simple.** It's better to have two strong numbers than ten weak ones (nobody will read them anyway).

Remember: if you have big-issue data, the eyes of the top team will be on you.

Excursion: Can You Give Your Big Customer Issue a *Number* with Simple Data?

We believe you can. The Net Promoter Score (NPS), for example, is based on asking customers just one simple question: How likely is it that you would recommend this company or brand to a friend or colleague? The answers provide a simple currency everyone understands, that can be used across all customer touch points (e.g., call centers, shops) and company units.

One marketing leader has even installed live screens in the office to display customer feedback from stores, call centers, and websites. The company continuously learns about longer-term customer issues and can also react quickly if shorter-term problems appear.

Inevitably, tools like NPS oversimplify reality, so some marketers—and, especially, market researchers—reject them on technical grounds. But that's missing the point. Your aim is to get people focused on profitably meeting customers' needs better than the competition, starting with reducing the drivers of customer dissatisfaction. Really simple tools like NPS (followed up with more sophisticated research) can help you achieve that.

Don't Ask for a Promotion. Ask to Lead the Big-Issue Resolution Team

Once you've identified a big issue for customers and the CEO inside the V-Zone, you need to make your case for how you want to solve the issue, so that the senior leaders entrust you to lead the execution of the plan.

Asking to lead the big-issue resolution is exactly what Sonya,* the new marketing manager for a US broadband company, did.

Her first weeks in the company made it clear: marketing wasn't a happy place. When she asked her team about life in the company, one brand manager said, "No one takes marketing seriously." Another complained, "All they do is cut our budget." The marketing department was working in a silo, isolated.

To make marketing relevant again, Sonya knew she had to get her team to focus on a big issue, and she had to take the lead. But what was the issue?

At the time, every brand in the fast-growing market seemed to have only one goal: capturing new customers through deals. Shops everywhere were plastered with alluring offers for broadband contracts. But Sonya soon discovered that buyers hated having to worry about the "best deal." Many just wanted a good (simply better) contract that they could then put out of their mind and not think about.

Sonya also learned that the company spent huge sums on getting new customers but did little to retain the profitable ones they had. This practice was digging them into a hole, especially since the market was maturing and the number of new broadband adopters was slowing, and the CEO was getting nervous about long-term profitability.

Sonya concluded that the company had to change its entire customer model from numbers-driven acquisition to more selective acquisition and market-leading retention. She did some scenarios based on her proposed new model, and even the conservative ones showed the company could save US$2.5 million every month if they retained customers better.

Of course, the road ahead for Sonya wasn't smooth. Changing how the company acquired and retained customers would touch many

---

* Name and context have been changed.

departments outside marketing, like operations and sales. She faced some spirited arguments about how marketing was failing and met leaders who wanted to shift the responsibility for the company's ailing performance onto everyone else. At one operations meeting, for instance, Sonya threw gasolene on the fire by bluntly telling everybody how the company did it wrong (not realizing the extent to which her message put people on the spot).

The more she spoke with board members, however, the more interest they showed in her bold plan. The breakthrough came at a year-end management meeting. Sonya had refined her strategy based on coworkers' input. She took a deep breath, presented her plan, and in the end said, "I'm happy to step forward and lead this transition."

The meeting went well. At the end of her presentation, the CEO stood up and said, "You have fully convinced us. I want you to revamp our customer strategy."

Within two years, the company had changed its entire marketing model. Profit margins recovered. And as existing customers felt better treated, customer satisfaction grew as well. Sonya hadn't just gotten a promotion. She led a big-issue resolution team that expanded the V-Zone.

Asking to lead the team that tackles a big issue is an effective way for marketing leaders to rise up the organization. In the research for this book, it was striking how many successful marketers had made significant career steps by asking to lead a big-issue resolution.

One CMO of a consumer goods firm is another example for how tackling a big issue creates the platform for stepping up.

When she joined as a brand manager, the company had no CMO. After leading her first large projects, in which she could prove herself, she started to develop a vision of what future marketing in the company needed to look like. The market was changing and digital marketing was a huge opportunity. She had a vision for how the company should serve consumers in the future. But she was also convinced that only a real CMO could steer the required digital transition.

She developed her plan and presented it at a board meeting, together with a suggestion to become the CMO. The board agreed.

This newly promoted CMO, too, expressed her career ambitions in a very smart way. She had identified a big issue inside the V-Zone ("serving customers digitally"), developed a plan to tackle it, and offered to lead the execution of that plan. This big-issue approach laid the foundation for her career as a highly accomplished CMO.

Marketers often admit that they don't like to ask for the next promotion. However, our research suggests that actively pursuing your career aspirations in the right way does help to drive career success. Don't just ask for a promotion. Instead, develop a well-thought-out plan to expand the V-Zone and then offer to lead the implementation.

Excursion: Leading the Big Digital Issue

For most CEOs today, digital strategy is a big issue. Marketing leaders could play a prominent role in helping their companies shape the digital strategy—and ultimately help serve customers better. But the most common feeling "digital" produces in marketers is fear. Fear of not knowing enough. Fear of missing a key trend. Fear of appearing to be behind the curve. One CMO told us, "Digital drives me crazy. All these darned new tools I'm supposed to learn. There are ten more each day. My CTO has just bought some new data mining software and I need to come up with a view on how we could use it to extract more value from our customer data. It never ends."

Shaping the digital strategy is complex—but it's doable. Unfortunately many marketers confuse digital strategy ("how could digital help us expand the V-Zone?") with tactics ("which digital tools should we use?"). That's like choosing a car color before knowing you need a car in the first place.

Zooming between strategy and tactics—without confusing them—is a key muscle every marketing leader must stretch.

It's OK, for example, for a young marketer to "zoom in" on key digital tools and techniques. But once you're managing a team—never mind

(continued)

the whole marketing function—you can't possibly stay in permanent "zoom-in" mode and learn all the new digital tactics. You'll never make it and—worse—you'll miss the chance to help your company with something even more critical: defining the digital customer strategy.

As a marketing leader you must first "zoom out" and shape the strategic digital customer agenda. This means answering one big question: *How can digital help increase the V-Zone*—meeting customer needs *and* company needs? Only then should you zoom back in on the specific combination of tactical tools to deliver the strategy.

Zooming out and then in (and then maybe out again, and so on) is how the best marketers ensure that "digital" is creating value.

If you feel you aren't on top of digital, you are not alone: no one is—apart, perhaps, from a few pure-play digital-only businesses. But the following steps should help you get ahead of the digital strategy curve, whatever your seniority level.

Zoom Out

Before looking at specific digital tools, step back and ask yourself:

1. How could digital help solve a real (known or latent) *customer* need (e.g., getting the product to the customer faster, cheaper, more tailored, or more conveniently)? How can digital help us improve the quality of the product or service itself, or any other aspect of the customer's experience?

2. How could digital help tackle a real *company* need (e.g., inventing, making, distributing, or selling products better, faster, more efficiently, or more profitably)?

3. How can digital enlarge the *V-Zone* (the overlap between customer needs and company needs)?

4. What should your company's digital customer strategy be, based on steps 1–3? Team up with your CTO, CFO, or COO and maybe a select group of external partners to shape this strategy. In these debates, you'll soon see which external partners just want to sell you stuff (maybe the majority) and which can genuinely help

you develop the strategy. Ask two or three external advisers to do a digital diagnosis for you. Develop a view on timings, costs, and feasibility. In our experience, the whole process could take three to six months. Perhaps you will—after your analysis—find that the biggest growth and profit levers for digital are customer insights for innovation, or speed of production, or even—yes it's possible—advertising and promotion.

5. Shape the digital customer strategy debate. As you'll learn in this book, a "great answer" doesn't mean people will automatically follow you. Implementing your digital strategy will almost certainly involve many people from outside marketing. You'll need to discuss your proposals with all the key stakeholders, ideally by involving them in creating the strategy. Plan for another three to six months of walking the halls before you get real traction (see also Section II, Power #5). The good news is that you'll now have a clear digital perspective and this will set you apart.

Zoom In

Strategy is key, but you also need to understand—in sufficient depth—the most important tactical digital tools for your strategy. Since you now have a strategic perspective, you should be able to eliminate most of the constant stream of digital tools that come your way and concentrate on the more doable and useful task of going deep on a few. Here's how:

1. Select just a few (two or three) digital tools or tactics in line with your strategy for implementation. Either implement them directly or pilot them. Get some *street knowledge* too. Use the key instruments yourself for a while, get training, get your hands dirty. Even if you're the CMO. Zooming in will come in very handy when you have to make bigger decisions about these tools—because you'll have been there. Using most of these tools isn't rocket science, and getting into two or three of them is perfectly feasible

(continued)

if you spend a bit of time on it. The key thing about zooming in is to be very, very selective.

2. Cull the rest. To make digital work, you'll have to bet on a few horses. If your digital roadmap has twenty-five instruments and tools, you'll likely do nothing well. Pick the two or three most critical (see number 1). Drop most of the rest and put just a few others aside that you *may* want to revisit.

3. Decide what to outsource. If you can't yet prove the impact of a digital instrument, try to have someone external run it for you on a trial basis, look at results, and then decide. Many people will try to sell you tools. The better strategy is to have someone run the tool for you for a while, and when you are convinced, buy it.

4. Do the numbers. If a digital instrument is really working, you should have the numbers (profit, revenue). If you can't get at least broad-brush numbers, you and others are probably kidding yourselves about the tool's effectiveness. Most digital marketing tools aren't about long-term brand building but about relatively fast, granular, measurable customer responses and other short-term, measurable results.

5. Pilot one instrument completely "off agenda." We have just told you that strategy determines which tactical tools you'll choose. Now for a contrary piece of advice: test one tool that may be totally off strategy but that you find interesting. In a fast-moving digital world, you can't foresee everything. It's OK to play with one new instrument at the side, see its results, and, if they're encouraging, zoom out and adjust the strategy. Since you now have an overall focus, you can allow yourself a little distraction. Rumor has it that this is how Google developed some of its most profitable innovations.

Zooming in and out will help you shape the important digital customer strategy—and master the key digital marketing tactics. Your strategic perspective, paired with firsthand tool knowledge, even at the highest level in your company, will help you shape the digital debate. And that—we know—is what most CEOs expect their marketers to do.

As a marketing leader, ensure you only tackle big issues inside the V-Zone. When in doubt, follow the advice of Jill McDonald, a former CMO who became CEO of motoring-related retailer Halfords: "Always take yourself back to the raw principles of being in business—how are you making money; what do your customers think about you?"

Critical Questions You Must Answer

To claim your seat at the top table and to mobilize your boss for your customer agenda, you must tackle a big issue, one that increases the overlap between customer needs and company needs. Tackling a big issue is at the heart of your drive to expand the V-Zone.

- What are your customers' top needs?
- What are your company's senior leaders' top needs?
- How can you prove that the big issue is big, using a price tag based on credible data?
- How can you ask to lead the effort to tackle the big issue?
- Are you zooming in and zooming out enough to lead the digital strategy debate in your company?

You can also download these questions here: www.marketingleader.org/download

| | | | |

Deliver Returns,
No Matter What

Your central question:

Am I cost or revenue?

As a marketing leader you must constantly prove that marketing delivers financial returns. Why? If the organization knows your work delivers a return, the decision makers will give you additional money for your important marketing projects.

To better understand what we're talking about, let's look at the work of former Ford CMO, Jim Farley.

Soon after Jim left Lexus to join the company in 2007, Ford, like most US car manufacturers, got hit by the financial crisis. Its already slowing sales nosedived, and in 2008 Ford was posting major losses.

Jim knew that brand preference had a big influence on purchases, and that Ford's image was in tatters. He felt that the best way to regain market share was to rebuild the organization's once-hallowed brand. Doing so, however, would take time and money.

As you can imagine, many of Ford's leaders were skeptical. Cash was tight and company managers were reluctant to spend on marketing, which they said had uncertain outcomes. Jim faced a major challenge: proving that marketing works.

With colleagues in finance and other departments, Jim created a model that showed how brand preference drives sales. The model wasn't perfect, but it was good enough to show the links between marketing investments, brand preference, and sales.

Jim then toured the globe. He sat down with the managers of each major market and shared the model. Because the model was developed with input from finance, people generally trusted the numbers. But, of course, the model also used estimates, which opened the room for debate. Jim took the time to listen to all concerns. He didn't shy away from the discussion, and in the end he managed to convince Ford leaders about the effects of marketing.

A CEO from one of Ford's international offices told us, "Jim was passionate but also serious. He wouldn't leave the room until he had addressed all our concerns."

For the first time, a wide range of leaders in Ford understood how marketing helps drives sales. Over time managers agreed to invest again in brand-preference building and other marketing activities. It was the start of a remarkable recovery, which made Ford the preferred choice for many buyers again.

Delivering and proving marketing returns is essential if you want to mobilize senior leaders to fund your important activities.

"As a marketing leader, I must accept the burden of proof that our activities create value for the company," said Benjamin Karsch, CMO of cosmetics firm Revlon, when we asked him about the importance of return orientation.

A key phrase in Benjamin's quote: "burden of proof."

Contribution to Marketers' Business Impact and Career Success

Business	Deliver Returns, No Matter What (12%)
Career	Deliver Returns, No Matter What (3%)

Variation in marketing leaders' perceived business impact and career success accounted for by this power as a percentage of the total variation accounted for by all 12 Powers in the neural network model (N = 1,232). In our research, what constitutes "Deliver Returns, No Matter What" includes behaviors and traits like return orientation (foremost), but also analytic thinking and displaying strong principles.

The Marketer's DNA-study, Barta and Barwise, 2016

In our core research, delivering returns was a big driver of marketers' business impact (12 percent contribution) and also contributed, at the margin, to their career success (3 percent).

The results make sense: when you spend your money well to attract profitable customers, the business grows. And when you produce visible returns, you are more likely to get more funds—which in turn creates even more revenue and profit. It's a pretty simple equation.

Marketers struggle with return orientation. Only two-thirds (67 percent) of the marketing leaders in our study said they had a strong return orientation. Most company leaders would say that that's an overestimate: for instance, over 50 percent of C-suite executives in a recent study didn't think that the company's marketing expenditure was even significantly driving top-line revenue, never mind bottom-line profits.

In other words: your CEO may not trust that you're spending the money well.

Saying marketers don't spend the money well is partly unfair. Marketing's impact on revenue, for example, can be hard to measure, especially for investments in long-term brand building.

But many marketers could do a much better job showing how their work drives revenue and profit. This includes *measuring* the revenue effects that are easy to quantify and *explaining* those that are harder.

If you take your boss's perspective, you'll immediately see why proving your returns is essential.

In a nutshell, CEOs are concerned with *strategy* (where to take the company), *organization* (people, skills, etc.), *revenue* (the current and future top line), and *cost* (the other determinant of the bottom line).

What happens if your boss doesn't associate you with *revenue*? Well, in that case, you're just a *cost*—and, in the words of Andy Duncan, CEO of lottery operator Camelot, "Marketing can . . . be seen as a cost rather than an investment, which is cut when businesses face difficult times."

The Revenue Camp

Get into the revenue camp. That's what the most successful marketing leaders do—in the minds of company leaders and also in reality. Delivering revenue and returns takes more than running great campaigns.

In the upcoming few pages we'll share a number of proven ideas for how you can get into the revenue camp. Examples will include how to make your work more transparent, estimate returns, pick the right marketing instruments, and behave as an investor.

Not all of these ideas may fit your individual situation. It's for you to pick the ones that will benefit you the most. Let's take a closer look at some of these ideas.

Align on How Marketing Works

"It's our job to help company leaders understand what we do as marketers," says Anna Bateson, Director, Global Consumer Marketing at YouTube. Her words couldn't be truer.

Marketers often assume everybody knows how marketing works. But most people don't; at least not in a way that's meaningful. That's why it's your job to ensure people understand what marketing does and how it's driving the business.

Many marketing leaders, like Jim Farley, have greatly benefited from explaining to the organization how marketing works with a simple model.

Figure 2.1 The Marketing Funnel

Stages of a decision and purchase process (simplified)

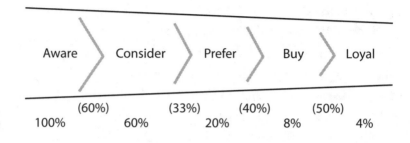

| People | 100% | (60%) 60% | (33%) 20% | (40%) 8% | (50%) 4% |

Simple is the keyword. A marketing model that everyone under-stands is worth ten times more (for this purpose) than a complex one that nobody gets. As a sophisticated marketer, the simplification we suggest here may make your heart bleed. Our advice: get over it.

One example of a simple model is the marketing funnel. Using it allows you to say things like, "Only 20 percent of people prefer our brand. We need to increase brand preference, because 40 percent of all who prefer us end up buying us."

By showing how, in the eyes of others, marketing concepts like *preference* have a big impact on *sales,* you'll significantly increase the leadership's understanding of your work and how marketing helps the business.

Sholto Douglas-Home, CMO of international recruitment firm Hays, for example, successfully uses a three-part marketing model of awareness, acquisition, and engagement to help company leaders decide on investment priorities. Sholto's advice for marketing leaders: "To engage senior management in marketing, use clear business-oriented language."

Make sure you build these marketing models together with people from outside of marketing (especially people in finance and sales) to give the models validity, credibility, and supporters.

Once you have an agreed-upon model, share it widely. Don't shy away from taking comments or having a debate.

Each time we propose models like this we get lots of pushback from marketers (never from CFOs): "not a good picture of reality"; "useless in a digital age"; "too simple" (to quote just the nicest ones). We hear you—intellectually. These types of analyses oversimplify reality and will never be perfect. But everyone understands that.

It would be great if you could find a nice, complex, and accurate model that everyone still understands. Feel free to try (and please send us a copy). But your bias should be to keep things simple. You may be surprised at how powerful a really simple model like this can be as the basis for discussion with other departments.

Ford, Hays, Anheuser-Busch InBev, and many others use simplified models for their internal communication. You can do it too.

Open the Books

"Dear James,* Sorry I couldn't reach you personally. Over the last two months we have benchmarked our advertising costs. As a proportion of revenue, our company spends almost twice as much on advertising as our largest competitor. That's unacceptable. I've decided to cut this year's advertising budget by 35 percent and next year's by a further 10 percent. I'm sure you'll understand our need to manage costs. It's a tough year for us."

In closing his CFO's email, marketing director James could feel the heat rising inside him. "Bean counter! He didn't even ask me!"

James, marketing head for a US sports brand, recalled the endless budget debates with finance. He was tired of having to discuss marketing funds each time the company had a bad month.

But this time he had an idea: "If you can't beat them, join them." The next day, James took the boldest move of his career. He met with the CFO and proposed setting up a joint team to evaluate the effectiveness of all marketing activities. Open book. No hiding.

The CFO was surprised and, after some hesitation, agreed. The project ended up changing everything.

---

* Name and context have been changed.

The joint marketing and finance team found that most campaigns did create a decent return. There was some scope for shifting resources (although some highly profitable activities, such as search engine optimization, couldn't be scaled up much).

Other activities generated significant learning and were therefore useful. But some others, including two high-profile sponsorships, created neither returns nor learning. The team decided to stop them completely. They subsequently also worked out together how to best measure and report marketing success.

"At first, the process was painful," James told us, but he said opening the books made marketing more relevant and influential. Some of the budget cuts were reversed. More important, people in the organization finally understood how marketing drove the bottom line.

Head of Customer Abigail Coomber, at British Airways, says, "CMOs need to show the ROI of every penny spent on marketing and how it delivers against the bottom line." She, like many leading marketers, agrees that opening your books is among the most powerful things you can do to prove returns.

There's no shortage of tools and books on how to measure marketing returns.* This is a leadership book, so we won't talk about measurement per se. But as many marketers struggle to install a sensible return measurement system (and most CEOs complain about it), let us share what some of our clients have done:

1. **Measure what's big.** Measuring the return on some smaller items may cost you more than it's worth. Take a look at your overall budget. Identify the big and critical items. Focus on measuring these first.

2. **Get finance involved.** Work with your experts from the finance team to jointly define and agree how you want to measure returns.

---

* See also the database of almost 10,000 marketing effectiveness cases at www.warc.com. These can be searched by industry sector, country/region, campaign objectives, media, budget, target audience, etc.

You'll find that most finance professionals understand very well that not everything can or should be measured. But problem solving this jointly will greatly increase the credibility of your numbers.

3. **Take an 80/20 approach.** Marketing measurement isn't about getting every penny right. Some activities like brand PR, for example, are pretty hard to evaluate (or rely on many assumptions). Some people use sophisticated econometric models alongside more behavioral measures, considering short- and long-term effects and measures of changes in brand strength. Others do very well with a simple quarterly spreadsheet that has marketing spend and sales. If you're unsure, invite three agencies or experts to present how they would set up your marketing measurement system. Get a simple one to work first—and expand it later.

4. **Show your returns frequently.** This can feel scary, but sharing your estimated marketing returns with top management is one of your best ways to build credibility as a leader. Crucially, sharing returns includes sharing the failures.

In our experience, marketing leaders who open the books get more support for marketing investments.

Get Involved in the Most Powerful Marketing Instruments

Daniel,* a CMO, had a problem: he wasn't getting his boss's attention. A regional marketing head of a large consumer electronics company, he often found himself last on his boss's agenda. Daniel isn't alone. Millions of marketers struggle to get attention. Perhaps the company doesn't see their work as critical.

Evidence on whether marketing's influence is increasing or decreasing is mixed, but every marketer would like it to be greater. In a recent study by the University of Mannheim, top executives rated pricing,

---

* Names and context have been changed.

Table 2.1 What Marketers Do (Percentage of Respondents)

	Responsible*
Communication	77
Brand development	63
Product development	56
Sales promotion	55
Customer retention	55
Corporate strategy	39
Sales	38
Pricing	32

* Concerned with on a day-to-day basis
The Marketer's DNA-study, Barta and Barwise, 2016

product development, and strategy as the most important business functions. Unfortunately, marketers weren't seen as very involved in these.

Our study paints a similar picture: just 32 percent of senior marketers claimed to have a stake in pricing, 39 percent in strategy, and 56 percent in product development. They were more likely to be involved in activities such as communication (77 percent), seen as less important by the Mannheim top executives. That's perhaps unfair (and incorrect). But perception is reality. If people think your work isn't important, you won't be seen as important.

Thomas recalls, "Before Daniel (the consumer electronics CMO) became a client, I asked him, 'What do you do?' He replied, 'I look after our brand and brand communication.' Even as the head of marketing, Daniel had stayed away from the big profit drivers—pricing, product, distribution, and strategy. And when I interviewed senior leaders at Daniel's company, many described him as a 'lightweight.' No wonder he didn't get attention."

As part of a six-month program, here are three steps Daniel took to ensure he started influencing the most powerful marketing instruments:

- **Step #1. Find the company's biggest growth levers.** If you help the company grow profitably, you'll be in the game. Daniel figured out that distribution was a major bottleneck. Competitors were simply in more shops. Another big issue was pricing. The company adjusted prices almost daily to steer product sales in a tough market. But the process was unsophisticated, and cutting prices too much immediately hit the bottom line.

- **Step #2. Throw the biggest stone.** Once you know the big growth levers, go where you can make the biggest difference. In Daniel's case, the head of sales had just hired two pricing specialists. It didn't—at this point—make sense for Daniel to tackle pricing. Distribution was a bigger opportunity. Daniel knew the retail landscape and already had ideas about how to get products into more stores. Distribution was the way to go.

- **Step #3. Start small, think big.** As a marketing leader, when you engage in a new field, take small steps but have the end in mind: long-term profitable growth. Daniel knew he couldn't just jump into distribution. Instead, he did his homework. First, he collected the company's distribution information. He found the data to be patchy—nobody had a full overview. His team created a dashboard, showing that dollar-weighted distribution was only at 68 percent of stores. With these insights, Daniel got more involved. His team developed distribution ideas and even shifted the marketing budget to fund these efforts. One day he felt comfortable enough to share his vision: "Let's crack 80 percent." The sales team initially felt put on the spot. But with data in hand, people listened to Daniel. Eighty percent became the goal. When it was reached, a big part of the success was credited to Daniel.

It took Daniel several weeks to get into the revenue camp. Now, lack of attention, for him, is a thing of the past.

Your influence as a marketing leader goes up when you work on the company's biggest issues and help increase the V-Zone. Getting involved in what matters may take you several steps. How about taking the first step today?

Ask yourself: Do you work on the right marketing instruments to be influential?

Be the Guardian of Customer Surplus

Is there a gap between what your company offers and what customers are happy to pay for? This gap is called customer surplus—the difference between the value customers are getting from your offer and how much it's costing them. The bigger the customer surplus, the more satisfied customers will be (although it may also mean you could increase your prices). You should know all about your customer surplus if you want to help your company serve customers profitably. Here are three ideas that can help:

1. **Find out what customers really value.** Techniques such as conjoint analysis (where customers trade off product features against each other and against price and brand) can help, as can other research techniques such as depth interviews or small-scale in-market tests.

2. **Know the real cost of options, features, and benefits.** Try to understand the true incremental cost to your company of adding extra features and options (including indirect costs). Similarly, explore the direct and indirect cost savings from *cutting* features and options— perhaps drastically—which can be a powerful strategy, as shown by the best low-cost airlines and retailers. At higher price points, a narrow product line, such as Apple's, can also make things easier for customers by not offering them too much choice. That means you'll need to work closely with operations and possibly other functions (sales and service, HR, IT) as well as, obviously, finance.

3. **Debate the customer surplus.** Some of the most respected marketing leaders discuss customer surplus issues regularly within the company. The CMO of a tool maker told us: "I always update one chart with the price and costs of our tools, what customers are ready to pay, and which features they really use. It has taken me over a year, but now everybody looks at my numbers—and everybody asks for my advice."

Act Like an Investor

"To the Shareholders of Berkshire Hathaway Inc.: Berkshire's gain in net worth during 2014 was $18.3 billion, which increased the per-share book value of both our Class A and Class B stock by 8.3%. Over the last 50 years (that is, since present management took over), per-share book value has grown from $19 to $146,186, a rate of 19.4% compounded annually."

The first two sentences by Warren Buffett in Berkshire Hathaway's annual report leave no doubt about what matters to Warren's shareholders: returns. You'll have to look very long and hard to find a marketing report that talks a similar language.

Successful marketing leaders act like investors—and people see it. They treat their budgets like investment money and have no problem asking for more—or less—if the opportunity is right. They "focus investments to where they make the most meaningful customer connections," as Hershey's CMO Peter Horst says. These marketing leaders, in the minds of their superiors, are in the revenue camp.

Our research shows: taking an investor mindset and creating returns is key for your business impact.

Here are some strategies you could consider:

Invest Less

Really? As a marketer, the company gives you funds. It's your job to create returns with these funds. If your analysis suggests that a marketing activity isn't at least covering its costs, cut it. Redeploy the resources or even give the money back. That will make people sit up!

Remberto Del Real, head of Commercial and Business Banking Marketing for BMO Harris Bank, told us how he discovered a six-figure budget for golf events in his first week on the job. He knew that these events generated client entertainment opportunities for the sales force, but he asked his team, "Does this generate a high return on marketing expenditure?" The answer was no. He transferred the budget to sales, since they were better placed to generate returns from it. Remberto had—overnight—increased trust in marketing across the top team (and won some new friends in sales).

Invest More

Like any investor, you may at times find opportunities that promise high returns. Remember, the company wants to find profitable investments. In fact, most companies are constrained by a shortage of good investment opportunities (although there are plenty of bad ones), not by a constraint on capital. If you can show a convincing, evidence-based case for investing more, every good CFO will listen and try to find the money you need. "Marketers are sometimes too fixated on their existing budget," one CFO told us, wondering why his CMO never asks for funds if a great opportunity comes up.

If the opportunity is right, asking for a bigger budget can be powerful. One of our CMO clients recalls that, after joining her company, she found that offering home insurance policies to customers just before the winter holiday period generated over 50 percent more uptake than usual. The timing seemed right—but her predecessor had already spent his annual budget. She did the numbers, called a board meeting, and got the extra budget signed off on in twenty-five minutes.

As a marketing leader, you're an investor. That sometimes means investing more—if you can make the case.

Do More with Less

General Mills, under then-CMO Mark Addicks, launched Fiber One yogurt on a shoestring budget spent mainly on a social media campaign. Among many activities, they had Hungry Girl (a well-known weight management blogger) send daily emails to her one-million-plus fans. The low-budget launch worked and laid the foundation for a very successful new product line.

Many substantial brands have been launched with tiny budgets— Nutro dog food, Glacéau Vitaminwater, Proactiv skincare, among others.

The good news is that small budgets call on marketers' core strength: creativity.

We often advise marketing leaders to cut budgets for some activities or some parts of their team, to trigger creative ideas.

You'll be amazed how well small budgets can work.

Do Less—But Big

Marketers often spread budgets and creative efforts too thinly across too many things, especially since the proliferation of new digital marketing options. You create the biggest splash by throwing one big stone into the water—not by throwing lots of small ones.

John Bernard told us, "As head of marketing for LG Mobile, my boldest move was to put 80 percent of the entire budget behind the launch of one new product: a handset called Chocolate. There was fierce internal debate. People naturally didn't want to reduce spending on other things."

Bernard won the argument and Chocolate became one of LG's most successful product introductions. Moreover, it showed how the whole marketing team, rather than fighting for their own patch, had acted like real investors for the company.

Great returns need focus. Aim to do a few things really well and on a big enough scale to make an impact.

Look at all your activities—are they really creating waves? If you are sponsoring, are you the most visible? On TV, do people notice you? At a trade fair, do you stand out?

Whenever you can: throw a big stone!

■ ■ ■

We have up to now shown you that, to mobilize your boss to support your marketing priorities, you must tackle only big issues inside the V-Zone and deliver returns—no matter what.

Let's now look at one more strategy to give you an additional advantage in mobilizing your boss: Power #3—working only with the best.

Critical Questions You Must Answer

Delivering returns is a key driver for your business impact. It will also help your career.

- Have you made clear to people in your organization how marketing works? What can and can't they expect of marketing?
- How can you open marketing's books to help people understand the returns you create?
- Are you working on the most important marketing instruments for the V-Zone—and how could you increase your influence on key revenue drivers?
- How well adjusted is the customer surplus your company is offering? Are you prioritizing the things that, relative to the cost of providing them, create the most value for the most customers?
- Do you have high-ROI opportunities for your current budget, or should you give some of it back?
- Are there high-ROI opportunities that would justify a higher budget, and have you explored this?
- Could you find significantly more effective ways to spend your budget (and perhaps even cut it in order to try)?
- Are you focusing on a few high-impact marketing activities rather than on many that are small?

You can also download these questions here:
www.marketingleader.org/download

| | | |

Work Only with the Best

Your central question:

Who are the best—and how can I work with them?

The way Steve Jobs led would, for many marketing leaders, be the fastest possible way out the company door. Jobs reinvented industries and changed how many of us work, listen to music, communicate, and so on. Yet he was described as hierarchical, aggressive, bullying, and intimidating—traits that, as our research shows, won't get you far as a marketing leader in a twenty-first-century organization.

But Jobs did a few things exceptionally well. One of these was that he spared no effort to find and work with the best people in their fields, no matter where they were—starting with brilliant computer engineer and Apple cofounder, Steve Wozniak.

In 1982, Jobs flew to Japan to secure advanced parts from Sony for his groundbreaking Lisa computer. Three years later, he paid top designer Paul Rand $100,000 for his NeXT company logo.

Working with the best—even if they don't live next door—isn't just what Steve Jobs did. RED, a small Danish consultancy, for example, is often credited with much of the success of German sporting goods maker adidas.

At McKinsey, project teams are routinely composed of experts from around the globe. The best people to help tackle a strategy problem at a client in Chicago might be based in the Johannesburg office. That's why the firm has removed all barriers for global staffing. *Where* someone is located is among the last things people care about in McKinsey and other top global firms.

Working with the best can transform your outcomes—but the changes on the way may take courage. That's the experience of Meng Whee,* a marketing director at a beverage firm in Asia.

Frustrated by the mediocre impact of her current marketing campaigns, she and her team started to scout for the best campaigns and agencies in her market worldwide. They found an agency in Brazil that was behind some of the most original and effective campaigns she had ever seen.

Meng Whee went to meet the agency's owner in Brazil. They immediately clicked. His ideas for her Asian market, where consumers buy and consume quite differently than in Brazil, were so compelling, she decided to hire him.

Her existing agency was outraged. The agency's owner called her one evening, threatening to talk to her regional manager, to get her fired, if she ended the relationship.

Meng Whee's regional manager and the agency owner were old friends. But Meng Whee stood firm. Instead of waiting, she set up a meeting with the regional manager and told him the evidence for why she believed that the new agency would be better for the business.

---

* Name and context have been changed.

Contribution to Marketers' Business Impact and Career Success

Business	Work Only with the Best (1%)
Career	Work Only with the Best (2%)

Variation in marketing leaders' perceived business impact and career success accounted for by this power as a percentage of the total variation accounted for by all 12 Powers in the neural network model (N = 1,232). In our research, what constituted "Hang Out with the Best," was a behavior described as "selecting the best external partners, independent of their location."

The Marketer's DNA-study, Barta and Barwise, 2016

The regional manager was torn—the agency owner was indeed a buddy. Yet, impressed by Meng Whee's determination and the examples of the Brazilian agency's work, he agreed to support her decision.

The new agency helped the company enter two new markets very successfully. Meng Whee's main brand, over a two-year period, increased market share by over 5 percentage points in a cutthroat market. Much of this was credited to better marketing campaigns.

She recalls, "Getting great new people to work for you can be risky, but I'd always do it again."

The benefit of working with the best external partners looks obvious. But too few marketers do it. Look for the best people—wherever they are.

When you take a closer look at our research data you may say: working with the best isn't such a major power.

On the surface, you are right. Compared to, for example, delivering returns, working with the best is less critical. But don't forget that in this book we are only showing powers with a statistically significant impact on success: many of the leadership items we tested didn't even make it into this book.

In the case of adidas (working with RED) and many other companies, working with the best led to breakthrough performance. In other words, if you can find the right partner, the results can be dramatic.

Only 62 percent of our marketing leaders even claimed to work with the best. Many simply prefer local partners and/or those they already know.

An argument we sometimes hear is: "We can't afford the best"—and the growing involvement of company purchasing departments is increasing the emphasis on cost rather than value. If that's you, take a second look. In the words of fashion designer Jil Sander, "People will forget the price, but they'll never forget the quality."

Working with the best isn't a straightforward budget question, it's a returns question. In a competitive and global market, you should work with the best people you can. If you succeed, you'll get a good financial return and, in turn, a stronger standing in your company (and people will forget the price).

Here's an important point, though: *the best* needn't be *the most expensive*. In fact, there's outstanding talent in small external agencies or partners. Don't look for the price tag—look for distinctive talent.

It's been said, "If you want to be famous, stand next to famous people." We admit that working with well-known top people may also help your internal brand as a leader, but this shouldn't be your main motivation to select the best. The only thing that matters is to work with those who can best help you deliver the best performance.

The best people to deliver what you need may not be in your city but in Cologne, Miami, or Seoul. Here are some ideas on how to find the best:

Look for Success

For every industry there are blogs and magazines that feature the best campaigns, products, and ideas. Get hold of these blogs and magazines from several different countries and review them with your team (but remember, some showcases are paid for and should be taken with a pinch of salt).

What are the best marketing campaigns internationally in your industry? Which external partners are behind these successes?

Go to Conferences—Not Just in Your Backyard

Many agencies and experts hang out at industry conferences, aiming to meet new clients. While some marketers may find this a pain, you'll often meet interesting people with good ideas.

Be open minded when you're approached at a conference (that's how adidas met RED). Go to meetings outside of your country too—you'll broaden your perspective, spark new ideas, and increase your insight.

Talk to New Partners from Time to Time

Loyalty to your existing partners or agencies is important. You want to build a strong relationship and establish common language and understanding.

But there's no harm in meeting new people a couple of times a year to stay current. Be fair and tell them that you may not be currently looking to replace your existing partners. And if you ask for ideas, show respect by paying for them. If you do, the partner will probably go overboard to make this a great meeting, hoping to win your business in the future.

Working with the best isn't rocket science. Is working with the best to create higher returns on your agenda?

■　■　■

Tackling only big issues, delivering returns—no matter what—and working only with the best will help you mobilize your boss, influence the company's customer agenda, and secure the resources you so urgently need to help the company grow.

In the next section we'll talk about how you can mobilize your colleagues. And as you'll see, this means activating a different set of muscles.

Critical Questions You Must Answer

Working with the best helps you mobilize your boss through delivering high returns and expanding the V-Zone.

- Which external partners have helped create the most impactful customer results globally in your industry (e.g. campaigns, products)? Are you in touch with them?
- Do you meet enough interesting new potential partners at, for example, conferences?
- How can you engage with new partners from time to time to calibrate the performance of your current external partners?

You can also download these questions here:
www.marketingleader.org/download

SECTION II MOBILIZE YOUR COLLEAGUES

"LEADERS MUST ENCOURAGE THEIR ORGANIZATIONS TO DANCE TO FORMS OF MUSIC YET TO BE HEARD."

—WARREN BENNIS

| | | |

Hit the Head and the Heart

Your central question:

How can I win my colleagues' hearts and minds?

As important as the marketing team is in creating a customer experience, it's only one piece of the puzzle. In almost all companies, the people who mainly determine the quality of the customer experience work outside of the marketing department.

To improve that experience, build long-term profitable growth, and enlarge the V-Zone, you'll need to mobilize your colleagues in all those other departments.

How, though, do you make that happen?

The trouble is that the colleagues in these other departments don't directly report to you. There are also lots of them, with many different agendas. To expand the V-Zone, you must find as much overlap as possible between the customers' needs, the wider company's needs, and your colleagues' needs.

Alexander Schlaubitz, CMO of German airline Lufthansa, summarized the challenge this way: "There's never been a better time for marketers to shape the customer experience at all touch points. It isn't so much about technology. It's a leadership challenge that requires understanding customer needs and mobilizing people across the organization to deliver real value for customers—and ultimately for the company."

Because you can't tell colleagues what to do, you must find other ways to mobilize them. And mobilizing others starts with sharing a vision that inspires them.

One of the best ways to communicate an inspiring vision is through a story.

For many years, we've taught clients and students about the importance of storytelling in leading a business.

But would storytelling come out as important in our core research? It did—and in a surprising way. Stories do contribute to marketers' business success (3 percent) but they matter more to their career success (7 percent).

The results tie into what many CMOs told us during interviews: a powerful vision helps the business and increases marketing's visibility inside the company.

Contribution to Marketers' Business Impact and Career Success

Business	Hit the Head and the Heart (3%)
Career	Hit the Head and the Heart (7%)

Variation in marketing leaders' perceived business impact and career success accounted for by this power as a percentage of the total variation accounted for by all 12 Powers in the neural network model (N = 1,232). In our research, what constitutes "Hit the Head and the Heart" is the behavior of communicating an inspiring business vision.

The Marketer's DNA-study, Barta and Barwise, 2016

Ford's former CMO, Jim Farley, went so far as to say, "Storytelling is your most important skill as a marketing leader."

To use stories effectively, of course, you don't have to be the high-profile CMO of a Fortune 500 company like Ford. In fact, many marketing leaders who succeed with stories work at less glamorous midsize firms that don't feature in the media much.

An example is Jaime,* a marketing manager whose customer vision helped turn around an ailing door handle business—not, you would think, a market to set the pulses racing.

It was the early 1990s. Making door handles was a tough, low-margin business—the product was seen as a commodity.

Jaime's company was one of the oldest US manufacturers in its field. Lower-priced Asian products were fast making inroads into a previously settled market. The company's founder, who was still in charge, had long refused to recognize the low-cost competition. "We beat them on quality" was his credo.

Unfortunately, more and more buyers, typically construction firms, found the lower-priced alternatives "good enough," and the company was writing escalating losses. A first round of cost cutting and layoffs had left deep marks with the long-standing staff.

Jaime was brought in by a restructuring consultancy to help turn the company's fortunes around. He spent his first weeks talking with staff, customers, and experts. What struck him: people inside the company had a lot of passion for door handles. "When you arrive at a house, the door handle is the first thing you touch," a worker told him. Another said, "I can tell your character from your home's door handle. It's like looking at people's shoes."

Buyers cared less. It was hard to get any interviews in the first place and all of them were short: "In the end, it's just a door handle," one buyer said.

Jaime kept digging. There must be an answer somewhere. He looked at the product pipeline for the next year. Higher quality and better

---

* Name and context have been changed.

materials. Not bad. Unfortunately, consumer tests came out at parity compared to the current models. Quality wasn't enough.

His idea for a solution came one day, as he took his pile of brochures to read into the company cafeteria. "Tired, young man?" the elderly cashier asked. "Yes," Jaime replied, "and I still have to read all of these."

"That must be boring," the cashier said. "All those door handles look the same."

"They do look the same," said Jaime. "That's the problem and the answer!"

The company had never thought much about door handle design. Jaime and his team worked with artists and designers to develop new, distinctive door-handle prototypes. The customer response to tests of about twenty designs was overwhelming. Designer door handles would not only sell . . . they'd yield significantly higher margins.

Even the CFO, who was skeptical about marketing, liked the plan and supported the launch of new design variants. But he also warned Jaime: "The old guy and many others here will hate this—they believe it's quality; nothing else."

The CFO's argument stopped Jaime in his tracks. What if the concept is right, the facts are right, but the executives simply don't want it? A friend suggested to Jaime to write a story. A compelling vision for the brand that addresses the facts but also captures people's hearts and gives them a chance to be part of it. Here's the kind of story Jaime wrote: "Our door handles are the first thing and the last thing people touch in a home. For generations, our products have been used by millions. Let's become the number one choice again. We can't compete on price. But customers told us how to win: let's make quality our hallmark, but let distinctive design be our new signature. Because when we do, customers will say, 'I want this one exactly—this feels great, and it looks great.' Price will be secondary. Let's all write history together. I need your ideas for how to make the best and the most attractive products again. Let's put our door handles back in people's hands."

Jaime's story worked. *Let's put our door handles back in people's hands* became an internal slogan. Staff across the company started to identify with his vision. The bright future he painted even persuaded the company owner to try the design route.

The new designs were a big success. Within two years, the ailing business had turned around. The company even ran designer contests and sold several limited luxury editions. Since Jaime's critical brand storytelling, designer door handles have long become an industry standard, copied by many competitors. All of this would probably not have happened without Jaime and his convincing story.

In most organizations, a top management decision doesn't mean things happen in reality. Think, for instance, about a new service. Employees from the service team, the sales team, and the operations team need to join the effort. Some may be skeptical. Some may even want to kill the idea—even if top management wants it.

As a marketer, you can't prove anything to your colleagues if they don't want to listen. But you can tell them a story. A story that captures their hearts and minds. A story that gets under their skin and mobilizes them to act.

People want leaders who give them hope, pride, an engaging idea, and some kind of higher purpose than just going to work for the money. You are tackling a big issue to expand the V-Zone. You need your colleagues to join you. Mobilizing colleagues starts with your story.

Find a story to help you mobilize your colleagues to serve customers better.

Here are some ideas for how you can find such a story.

Heart, Head, and How-To

So how can you write a story that captures people's imagination? By making sure you include three essential elements: heart, head, and how-to:

- **Heart: An inspiring vision.** As Napoleon said, "A leader is a dealer in hope." Your best story paints a hopeful—but attainable—picture of the future.

Ensure your story has a big aspiration that people can sign up for. In the door handle case this was "becoming the preferred choice again"; "writing history"; and, especially, the vivid imagery of people touching the product when they arrived at and left their home. Story examples like these get people's imaginations going.

But watch out: people can quickly turn cynical if your ideas aren't realistic. To motivate people, your vision needs to be inspiring but attainable.

- **Head: Credible evidence.** People may disagree with you—but no one can really disagree with customer data (at least not for long).

   There will always be naysayers. To counter them, make sure you have credible evidence, ideally from customers, that shows that your vision is achievable. Jaime used the customer responses to the product test to make his case "I want this one exactly."

- **How-To: Personal relevance for your colleagues.** Suppose you're a staff member listening to the leader's vision. Immediately you ask, "How does this affect me? What do I need to do?" Make sure your story answers these questions.

   Jaime showed the team how to win (by combining quality and design) and invited them to act by telling them, "I need your ideas for how to make the best and the most attractive products again."

P.S. Here's another nice example that caught our attention: when you've finished dining at Gitane, a small London restaurant, you receive a check that reads, "Love people, cook them tasty food." An inspiring story can be this short.

Use Customer Language Whenever You Can

As a marketing leader, you're the customer's voice in your company. Make sure you sound like it.

Don't say, "This TV ad doesn't match our brand guidelines." Instead, say, "As a customer, I'd be confused because this TV ad doesn't look like our previous ads."

Don't say, "Our product range has far too many SKUs." Instead, say, "As a customer, finding the right product would take me too long."

Don't even say, "We need to show our services charges more clearly." Instead, say, "As a customer, I'd hate to get a bill with hidden charges."

You get the point.

You'll be surprised at how easy it is to speak the customer's language—and how much more engaging you'll be while doing it.

Critical Questions You Must Answer

Mobilizing your colleagues begins with an inspiring customer story. Finding such a story is an important driver of marketers' career success and also contributes to their business impact.

- What's your inspiring customer story that will capture your colleagues' hearts and minds and help them understand how they can support the movement to increase the V-Zone?
- Are you using customer language when you communicate internally? Are you a true voice of the customer?

You can also download these questions here:
www.marketingleader.org/download

Walk the Halls

Your central question:

How can I get people moving?

Mobilizing colleagues to expand the V-Zone isn't a one-off activity—it never stops. You don't send an inspiring email and then you're done. To mobilize people, you get out of your office, share your ideas, listen to concerns, and create joint solutions—week after week, month after month, year after year.

Let's look at how some marketing leaders have mobilized their colleagues. We'll start with News Corp Australia's group marketing director, Ed Smith.

In early 2010, Ed had to handle an important problem: the company owned a slew of about 200 newspapers around the globe, like the *Wall Street Journal,* the *New York Post,* the *Times* (London), and the *Australian.* But all of those iconic titles were facing the same dramatic problem: a rapid decline in both advertising and subscription revenue, as readers and advertisers started shifting to free digital news. Given the high fixed cost of journalist-generated content, the revenue decline was a threat to their very survival. But that's not the half of it. News Corp was a highly decentralized business. Editors and divisional CEOs had huge power and autonomy. So there was no group revenue recovery effort. Each paper was trying its own recipe to stay profitable.

The management was convinced that, to survive, the company needed to start charging users for its online content. Ed's job, then, was to lead the introduction of paid content in the Australian market—News Corp's original heartland—to stem or recover the revenue losses and sustain the investment in quality journalism.

Ed recalls, "The initial pushback was massive. CEOs were nervous that pay walls would alienate readers. Journalists feared that quality would now be measured by how many people pay, as opposed to how good an article is. We had to create a common purpose first." Ed set up a series of meetings with the key decision makers. At each meeting, he first raised the company's purpose. Everybody agreed that, as a news company, they valued journalism that holds businesses, politicians, and others to account. Quality journalism underpins democracy, and the company must find ways of continuing to fund it. That got the dialogue going.

Then Ed listened to these leaders' concerns and ideas. Based on their input, and with support from senior journalists and other experts, he facilitated the development of a pay-for-content model.

But he didn't sit back and declare victory. Instead, he packed his bags again, went back for more meetings with the business leaders, and explained how and why their ideas had (or hadn't) been included in the final model.

From a starting point of doubt and disbelief, the paid digital business model project gained momentum and was implemented on time. It was a big success, particularly with the *Australian*, News Corp's premium quality newspaper in Australia—and served as a role model across the group and industry.

"The key is to meet with each individual," said another Group CMO. "Not via phone, not via email. To energize people, you need to sit down with them, share a vision, listen to their issues, and make them part of the solution."

The day when marketers have all the say in a company will never arrive. A nonnegotiable part of your job, then, is to mobilize your non-marketing colleagues, so the best marketing strategies—those that significantly enlarge the V-Zone—get championed and implemented. To achieve this, you need to keep walking the halls, talking to the leaders of every group that (directly or indirectly) influences the quality of the customer experience. And that's a lot of people, especially if you work in a large company. How do you get going? Well, why don't you start walking the halls in your office next Monday?

In our core senior marketer research, "Walking the Halls" was one of the largest drivers of senior marketers' business impact (13 percent of the total variation explained by the 12 Powers) *and* career success (also 13 percent).

Despite its importance, few marketers walk the halls as much as they should.

Only 52 percent of our senior marketers believed they mobilized colleagues well or deliberately acted as a role model.

Contribution to Marketers' Business Impact and Career Success

Business	Walk the Halls (13%)
Career	Walk the Halls (13%)

Variation in marketing leaders' perceived business impact and career success accounted for by this power as a percentage of the total variation accounted for by all 12 Powers in the neural network model (N = 1,232). In our research, what constitutes "Walk the Halls" is mainly the behaviors of energizing others to act and role modeling. Other related behaviors and traits like extroversion, openness, understanding one's own impact on others, and emotional resilience showed a measurable, yet very small, effect in the results.

The Marketer's DNA-study, Barta and Barwise, 2016

In our 360-degree database: only 59 percent of bosses said their marketers were good at mobilizing others and only 56 percent thought their marketers tried to be good role models. Both figures were lower than for any other type of functional leader, although the differences weren't huge.

And what did the marketers' direct reports think? Sixty-one percent of those direct reports thought their bosses were good at mobilizing others (slightly better than what the senior marketers' bosses thought). But when it came to role modeling, just 49 percent of team members thought their marketing bosses were good at it (once again, this was lower than the equivalent figure for any other function).

To summarize: Walking the halls to mobilize colleagues is one of the biggest success drivers for marketing leaders. Marketers don't think they're very good at mobilizing, and neither do their bosses and direct reports.

So there's considerable scope to do better. The good news is that walking the halls isn't complicated. Yet it does require sustained effort.

First you must accept that a core part of your role as a marketer is to mobilize colleagues. Second, you must develop a strong story, linked to a well-thought-out marketing strategy. Third, you must invest the time and effort to walk the halls.

As a marketing leader, you're expert in mobilizing customers. Use this expertise to mobilize colleagues too!

Here are some ideas that may help.

Share Your Customer Story Repeatedly and Consistently

As we discussed in the previous chapter, a powerful story is important. But don't tell your story just once. To make sure people get your point, you need to tell it over and over and keep it consistent.

You'd be surprised at how many marketers find it hard to tell a consistent story. A meandering message, however, creates problems.

Among all behaviors, skills, and personality traits, our senior marketers rated themselves highest on "open and creative."

Openness and creativity are great. These traits help you innovate and tackle wicked problems.

The downside is that openness and creativity can make it hard to focus. Some CEOs and peers of marketers told us they wished their marketing colleagues would be more selective about the messages they delivered.

Just as with brand communications, a strong, consistent main message for your colleagues is key.

Once you are clear about the big V-Zone issue you're tackling, shape your internal customer story (the vision you share with colleagues). Then it's all about repeating that consistent story, over and over.

To illustrate what we mean, meet Sony Ericsson's former CMO, Steve Walker.

In the early 2000s (before smartphones) the Sony Ericsson cell phone business was becoming stagnant. There were too many competitors selling similar products.

However, Steve, then head of product marketing, and his key partner, the head of product development, Rikko Sakaguchi, had an idea: Why not take Sony's iconic Walkman and combine it with a phone? In essence, they were putting music software on the upcoming phone models and using the well-known Walkman brand to communicate the music feature to customers.

Steve and Rikko shared the vision with colleagues. But walking the halls turned out to be difficult. Says Steve, "Everyone told us: 'Too difficult, too complex, too expensive.'" The development issues and legal considerations were too much to overcome—or so they were told.

Giving up wasn't an option for Steve. "For more than a year, we took every occasion to show people our dream," says Steve, "and what the product and brand would look like." Through sheer persistence, they gradually won over the skeptics.

In 2005, the W800 Walkman phone hit the market and was an instant success. At its peak, the phone contributed more than 25 percent of Sony Ericsson's global sales by value.

The lesson: walk the halls, keep your vision consistent, and don't give up. The tipping point may be just around the corner.

Listen, Decide, Communicate

More often than not, you'll be leading a marketing project that's not getting full agreement from the entire organization. How do you mobilize colleagues for large-scale change—even if that change might be seen as unpopular?

Use your secret weapon: LDC, which is "Listen, Decide, Communicate." We'll examine each step separately.

Listen

First, seek out the key people who'll be affected by the change and briefly summarize—not your project's details—but its overall goal. Then be quiet and listen closely to their views.

Listening is much more than catching every word. It's about understanding what's going on in the room. Mark Addicks, long-standing former CMO of General Mills, said, when speaking about the best advice he was ever given: "Be humble and be a good listener. When it was given to me the word *listen* meant really *observe*. A person I worked with said, 'Watch people. Watch their body language. Watch their level of commitment.'"

In particular, try to understand four things when you're listening:

1. Facts (What is this person's understanding of the facts?)
2. Feelings (How do they feel about the issue?)
3. Beliefs (What do they think is the proper course of action?)
4. Assumptions (What do they think will actually happen?)

To help you remember your key learnings, take notes.

Close the meeting by recapping what you've heard. Tell them what you intend to do next and when you'll get back to them.

Decide

Once you've gathered all the facts and views, decide on a course of action to take. In some organizations that means bringing together the leaders who need to make a formal decision, as CMO Ed did in our earlier News Corp case. However you do it, get it done.

Communicate

Once again, meet all the people from your first round. Tell them the decision that's been reached. Show how you've done your best to address their concerns. If you didn't choose their preferred option, explain why you didn't. It's crucial that they know they were genuinely listened to and their ideas considered. Close the meeting by thanking them for their contributions and asking for their support for the action plan.

Let's look at how LDC also laid the foundation for David James's biggest success as marketing director of BT (formerly British Telecom).

Whenever David had been convinced that an idea was right, he'd always tenaciously tried to persuade others to agree. One day, he'd even clashed about an issue with a nonmarketing colleague, at the same level as himself, in front of an entire management team. David won the argument, but the implications were severe: reduced support for marketing activities, tough debates over turf issues, and so on. In his own words, it was "a classic case of when it doesn't matter if you're right."

Over time, David learned that listening more to people, taking their concerns on board, and building alliances enabled him to achieve better outcomes.

The big chance to test this more collaborative approach arose in 2013, when BT launched a new TV offering, BT Sport, built on Premier League and Champions League football rights.

The leadership team expected BT Sport to do its main marketing push in August, just before the start of the new Premier League season. But David and his team had a different idea. To get ahead of the competition, they wanted to shift the timing and go big in May.

When senior management unsurprisingly challenged this bold suggestion, the marketing team decided to walk the halls. They met with people one on one, spelled out their vision and the data that supported it, listened to feedback, and tweaked their plans.

They shared the ownership of the idea—rather than just "selling" it. One by one, the key decision makers came around and became advocates.

The proposal was approved and BT Sport's massive early launch campaign left competitors stumbling. By the time they reacted, BT Sport's momentum was too great to stop. It signed up over 5 million subscribers in just over a year.

David says that the key to winning company-wide support was that, "Rather than telling people what to do, we presented an idea, let them shape it, and shared the success."

LDC is simply one of your most powerful techniques in mobilizing colleagues.

Make Work Cross-Functional

Each of us would like to be seen as a hero, but sometimes the best way toward heroics is by sharing responsibility and credit. For marketers, bringing other business functions on board is a top-notch formula for bigger and faster success.

Whenever you can, get colleagues from other departments to join your projects. You'll build a better network across the company and energize other departments in helping you to tackle big issues collaboratively.

Name the Elephant in the Room

When you walk the halls, you'll need to ensure that your conversations are meaningful. Among other things, that means not sweeping difficult issues under the rug. You want to identify and deal with those issues, especially the biggest ones.

Every company has big scary issues lurking in the background that no one wants to talk about—the proverbial "elephant in the room."

There are many reasons not to mention the elephant in the room. Perhaps it's so big that people think solving it is impossible. Or, maybe confronting it head-on isn't seen as culturally appropriate. Sometimes people don't talk about the elephant because they don't want others to perceive them as negative.

But if you don't try tackling—or at least naming—the elephant, you may get stuck before you've even begun.

In more forthright cultures, like the United States, the Netherlands, and Israel, people are more likely to say directly, "There's an issue we need to talk about." But we've also worked with leaders from more hierarchical and deferential cultures who know how to talk about the biggest stumbling blocks indirectly.

Want a smart way to name the elephant? Ask people, "What has to be in place for our plan to succeed?" Have them list all the important conditions they named. Then ask, "How can we put each of these conditions in place?" The debate will inevitably turn to the elephant without much effort. And you'll have framed it in a positive way designed to make things happen.

Naming the elephant doesn't mean you can always tackle it. Once it's named, though, you can at least problem-solve your way around it.

Rent a Bulldozer

You've walked the halls, told your story repeatedly and consistently, listened, decided, and communicated, made the issues cross-functional, and named and dealt with the elephants. You've built as much consensus as possible. Finally (with perhaps varying degrees of enthusiasm) the decision has been made to proceed with your critical project. That decision now needs to be *executed*.

For those types of key projects and decisions, you need the support of people who can force a way through the obstacles in your path.

In this situation, you should create a "war cabinet" of senior leaders with the clout to bulldoze through the roadblocks and keep the project moving.

Some of our clients set up regular phone or live meetings with their war cabinet. Others ask that their cabinet members be available within twenty-four or forty-eight hours.

Use your bulldozing cabinet members only when you must. But when you need them, explain the problem and refer back to the agreed plan. No one can challenge the agreed-upon plan without strong new evidence that the earlier decision was wrong.

Deal Smartly with GMOOT (Get Me One of Those)

Everyone, from the junior IT recruit to the chairman's spouse, seems to have a view on how marketing should be done. What do you do when a senior leader tells you her husband says, "Company X sponsors a soccer team and you should, too" or "Brand Y has N thousand Facebook followers. You need to match that" or some other version of "Get Me One of Those" (GMOOT)?

The more you walk the halls, the more you'll encounter the GMOOT problem.

In dealing with GMOOT, be patient and polite. Try to take the opinions you hear as helpful suggestions. At least they show engagement—and some may even be genuinely useful! As steward of the marketing budget, ask for evidence of the likely impact. If such evidence doesn't exist, you may be able to put the GMOOT to bed quickly.

When a GMOOT would potentially put your marketing effectiveness at risk, stand firm, say no, and explain why you're staying with your decision.

Most important: get used to it. The next GMOOT is probably right around the corner.

Share the Praise

Be sure to celebrate if you've hit a goal or major milestone. Publicly thank those who made things happen. Collect success stories involving contributors, and share them across the organization—including with the top team.

While this may not apply to you (ahem), our research told us that marketing leaders enjoy being the center of attention. That's OK. Remember, though: as a leader, your job is to energize *others*.

If the project succeeds, you'll automatically get credit as a leader!

Critical Questions You Must Answer

To mobilize your colleagues to expand the V-Zone, walking the halls is an essential power. It's an important driver of both business impact and career success. It's also an area where most marketers can take a leap forward. What about you? Try these questions:

- Do you share a simple, consistent customer story repeatedly, so that enough colleagues recall it?
- Are you walking the hallways —listening, deciding, and communicating (LDC)?
- Are you involving other functions in your projects?
- Have you named the elephants that hinder your company's success?
- Do you have a "bulldozer" to remove obstacles if your important customer projects get blocked or bogged down?
- Confronted with GMOOT, do you politely ask for evidence of relevance and effectiveness?
- Are you sharing praise with others, and are you doing so publicly and often?

You can also download these questions here:
www.marketingleader.org/download

| | | |

You Go First

Your central question:

How can I visibly act to increase the V-Zone?

However great your story, only tangible results will make you a successful marketing leader.

Not surprisingly, being seen as a conduit for tangible results is a top driver of marketers' career success (12 percent). It's also a significant contributor to their business impact (6 percent).

The reason is simple. The company's most senior leaders, who have a big say in marketers' career progression, value tangible outcomes, especially revenue and profit growth. No abstract idea, no story, no plan can compete with hard-nosed business results. The closer you speak and act on the revenue and profit lines, the stronger your internal recognition. And the more successes you create, the more colleagues will want to follow you.

Contribution to Marketers' Business Impact and Career Success

Business	You Go First (6%)
Career	You Go First (12%)

Variation in marketing leaders' perceived business impact and career success accounted for by this power as a percentage of the total variation accounted for by all 12 Powers in the neural network model (N = 1,232). In our research, what constitutes "You Go First" are mainly the behaviors of having clear action plans to drive the business and demonstrating marketing's business impact to colleagues.

The Marketer's DNA-study, Barta and Barwise, 2016

You are the movement. Your work is urgent . . . and people need to see this.

Let's look at how Greg,* a senior telecom marketing leader, showed everyone in the company how he helped drive the business.

One evening, Greg was working late when across the hallway a phone began ringing. He glanced at the display. The number was external, so his greeting was formal: "Good evening, my name is Greg. How may I help you?"

"At last!" responded the caller. "Your so-called helpline had me waiting for twenty-two minutes. I gave up and have been trying other numbers. Here's my problem: I'm in Mexico and someone just stole my phone! I need it tomorrow!"

"I'm so sorry to hear that," said Greg. He apologized for the delay, took the caller's address, and assured him that the company would do all that it could to help.

In reality, Greg had no clue how to get a phone to Mexico overnight. But he was determined to solve this customer's urgent problem.

Luckily, he found someone still working in the warehouse, and the replacement phone shipped within an hour of the call.

Greg had almost forgotten about the call when his social media team told him the next day: "You're a Twitter hero!" The customer turned

---

* Name and context have been changed.

out to be a rising rap star and told his 250,000 Twitter followers how a "Greg" at his phone company had saved his life—and that people should switch to this "freak'n cool company."

The news traveled throughout the organization, and in the coming weeks other colleagues tried to become heroes as well by retaining customers in unconventional ways.

Greg had won a loyal customer for life, generated some great word-of-mouth publicity, and started an internal movement for going the extra mile for customers.

So how can you mobilize colleagues by going first?

Start a Movement

If you have a good business idea, why not use it as the basis for a movement? Share your idea, show how it works, then—and this is key—find the first followers.

Starting a movement helped Tina Müller, who went on to be CMO of General Motor's Opel brand, create one of her largest successes as marketing head for cosmetics firm Henkel.

Tina launched the hair cosmetic brand Syoss, a range of consumer products developed with professional hairdressers. The Syoss concept was initially known only in the US market. Country managers were skeptical of its potential elsewhere. However, Tina managed to convince the country manager for Russia, who dared to launch it there. He was her first follower. The plan worked and quickly turned the skeptics into followers too. The brand is now successful around the globe.

Movements start with one leader taking a risk, trying something, and showing its effect. Then it's all about finding those important first followers.

If you want to start a movement in your organization, consider three steps:

1. **Ask yourself: What's my movement?** Look for an idea that's close to your customers' hearts, but choose one with wide potential

inside your organization, such as serving customers in a new way or getting a new product to market, so you are in the V-Zone (see also Power #1: Tackle Only Big Issues).

2. **Dare to go first by showing how your idea works.** As the leader of a movement, your role is to get up first. Show people how your idea functions in practice. When One2One manager Dee Dutta had the idea of prepaid mobile phone fees, nobody liked it. Dee got up and, through successful tests, proved his idea. It changed the industry. Getting up first is risky, but as a leader you need to be willing to take risks—and most people will respect you for doing so.

3. **Find those important first followers.** Once your idea is out, shift your focus and find followers who can start to fill the dance floor. This can happen literally, as at the 2009 Sasquatch outdoor music festival, when one guy started to dance—awkwardly yet joyfully. Hundreds of spectators wondered, What the heck is *he doing?* After a while, another brave guy joined the first dancer. Still, the crowd only watched. Then, a third guy joined in. This was the tipping point. Within minutes, people came running from everywhere, eager not to be left out. Finding the first followers is an underappreciated leadership skill, but it's crucial.

You can't be in charge of it all, but you can start a movement, so other motivated people take action on the idea's behalf.

Create Quick Small Wins

When it comes to building a movement, showing bosses and colleagues the result of a successful test is far more persuasive than sharing a well-reasoned, yet untested, marketing strategy document.

If you have an idea for tackling a big issue, prove it by running a small pilot as early as you can.

The marketing head of a US chewing gum maker saw that, in Asia, consumers were buying packages of gum that held forty or fifty pieces. In Europe, though, the largest gum packages held only ten pieces. When his colleagues didn't think it was possible to change the European paradigm, he conducted a small test and its success convinced the skeptics. Today, the forty-to-fifty-piece cans are well established and a major profit contributor.

Similarly, Kiyoshi Saito, general manager of Marketing Intelligence at Japanese telecoms giant Softbank, helped create a family tariff combined with a new phone-installment-payment scheme, which created the biggest wave of new subscribers the company had seen in years. It, too, started with a small-scale pilot. Once everyone saw that the concept could succeed, they banded together to make it happen at full scale.

Get to the Front Line

When your boss sees you going first in a way that bolsters revenue, your career is far more likely to succeed. You're seen as a mover and shaker. You're thought of as someone who is willing to roll up his or her sleeves to make things happen.

One way to be visible is to put yourself on the front line. How?

Pick up the phone and speak with a customer who complained. For a few days, spend time with the sales force. Work in the store and help sell.

Every year, board members of a supermarket group spend several days stacking shelves and serving customers at the checkout.

Getting to the front line isn't always easy. But it gives you a direct understanding of the mood among front-line staff and customers and what is and isn't working in the stores.

It also shows the front-line staff that you understand the importance of the shop floor in creating value.

Use Customer and Business Language (Not Marketing Speak)

Andy Duncan, CEO of Lottery operator Camelot, puts a big challenge for many marketers this way: "As a term, marketing is often misunderstood and too many marketers use jargon that other members on the board simply don't understand. As a result, marketing directors don't get taken seriously."

You need to walk the halls, but you should also talk the talk. Use words that people outside of marketing can relate to.

Your aim is to help the company increase the V-Zone. So use customer and business language.

The best type of language to use is customer language. In other words, talk about the things customers talk about and do so using their words.

The second best type is language that relates to your company's revenue or profitability: *sales leads, market share, product success, gross margins,* and so on.

As Singapore Post CEO Wolfgang Baier puts it, "The most respected marketing leaders keep their communication close to the revenue line."

Critical Questions You Must Answer

Talk is good—action that visibly drives the business is better; especially for your career. To mobilize your colleagues, find ways to demonstrate that your actions enlarge the V-Zone. That often means going first and showing what's possible.

- How can you start a movement in your organization by going first and by finding those important first followers?
- Are you creating some quick wins to prove your case?
- Are you visible at the front line and in ways that create immediate impact?
- Are you using the language of action (as opposed to the language of concepts and theories)?

You can also download these questions here:
www.marketingleader.org/download

■ ■ ■

Mobilizing your colleagues by sharing your inspiring story, walking the halls, and going first must be a big part of your day as a marketing leader.

Let's now see how you can increase your company's V-Zone by mobilizing the people who report to you—your team.

SECTION III MOBILIZE YOUR TEAM

"WHEN THE BEST LEADER'S WORK IS DONE THE
PEOPLE SAY, 'WE DID IT OURSELVES '"

—LAO TZU

| | | |

Get the Mix Right

Your central question:

How can I design and build the right team to increase the V-Zone?

A top priority for every marketing leader is to design and build a cohesive marketing team that can solve the big issues that matter both to customers and the company (V-Zone issues). This team will have cutting-edge skills and be a talent magnet for marketers outside the company and a talent pool inside the company.

If you've wondered throughout this book where functional marketing skills come into play, it's here! Building a well-aligned team with the right marketing *and* leadership skill mix is critical for your success. But, as we'll show you, getting the team's skill mix right is a challenge for many marketers.

Twenty-first-century marketing is suffering from a skills crisis. There's also confusion about priorities. In particular, the well-justified focus on digital and data skills means that other important areas are tending to be neglected.

Despite the burgeoning of digital media and data-based marketing, the basic role and nature of *strategic* marketing haven't changed.

Aligning with the CEO's priorities and the overall strategy; selecting the right target markets and customers; understanding customer needs; creating simply better, user-friendly products and services; developing engaging, cut-through communications; setting the right prices; and finding the right combination of distribution and customer support: all these are still at the heart of winning and keeping profitable customers.

Similarly, how to mobilize your nonmarketing colleagues to maximize the V-Zone and drive long-term business performance— everything we covered in the previous section—hasn't materially changed.

Tactical marketing methods and channels, however, are evolving fast and in lots of ways. Some traditional approaches, like TV advertising and many price promotions, haven't changed much* but the digital revolution is adding an ever-growing list of new ways to understand, target, reach, and support customers (social, mobile, big data, etc.).

Marketing departments are becoming more analytical and complex. This raises both technical and organizational challenges: you need to decide which marketing techniques to use and how to combine them in terms of structure and skills. For instance, what is the best way to optimize the skills of, and relationships between, the data analytics team, the market research team, outside suppliers of technology and insight, and those making marketing decisions?

McKinsey estimates[†] that by 2018 marketing teams in the United States alone will be short of close to 190,000 people with data analytics skills. Seventy-eight percent of CMOs expect more marketing

---

* Of course, things are evolving even here, e.g., because of the growth of online viewing and other types of addressability, but the pace of change is less than the hype about it. A visitor from thirty years ago would find little change in the role and nature of most TV advertising today.

† McKinsey & Company estimate, CSMO-Forum 2012.

complexity, but only 48 percent say they're prepared to deal with it. While all business functions face a digital skills challenge, marketing faces it in spades.

What's more, digital transformation is high on the agenda of CEOs. They expect their top marketers to play a big role in it.

Most marketers today feel swamped by all the new tactical marketing opportunities. In response, there are now more books, articles, conferences, seminars, and blogs to help them keep their functional marketing knowledge and skills up to date than ever before.

Too often, though, learning new skills takes too much energy away from a marketer's main task: coming up with and executing the ideas that drive customer-focused innovation and profitable revenue growth.

Their own and their team's skills are an issue for every marketing leader.

When you start out as a marketer, your priority is to develop your own functional marketing skills. But once you start leading others, even as a junior team leader, your role changes. Increasingly, it's about recruiting, developing, and motivating people with the right technical and human skills—the ability to listen, collaborate, keep going, etc. The best teams perform well, sustainably, and under pressure—without the leader's close supervision.

Many marketers find making the transition from marketing expert to marketing team leader hard. Why? Because they are used to being on top of the details and feel threatened by the increasing pace and complexity of what's happening. They find it hard to stay focused on the bigger picture and delegate the executional details to the technical experts on their team.

"You'll Never Walk Alone," the show tune from the 1945 Rodgers and Hammerstein musical *Carousel*, couldn't be truer for marketing leaders. Think about it: you want to change the customer experience that large numbers of people create each day in your company—most of whom don't work in marketing. You can't possibly achieve all this on your own. The only way to succeed is to become a "leader of leaders." Don't just build a support team. Build an influential team of marketing leaders to help the whole company to expand the V-Zone.

Contribution to Marketers' Business Impact and Career Success

Business	Get the Mix Right (20%)
Career	Get the Mix Right (7%)

Variation in marketing leaders' perceived business impact and career success accounted for by this power as a percentage of the total variation accounted for by all 12 Powers in the neural network model (N = 1,232). In our research, what constitutes "Get the Mix Right" are mainly analytical and creative skills of the marketer and his or her team, but also the leadership behavior of aligning the team to the company's business priorities.

The Marketer's DNA-study, Barta and Barwise, 2016

In this chapter, we'll take a deeper look into how you can build a team with the right mix of skills and ensure that they are aligned. In the following chapters we'll then show you how to coach and performance-manage your team. Doing all of this will help you develop and mobilize the most powerful marketing team for your organization.

How important are functional marketing skills for your business success? Very important. In our core research, getting the mix right (team skills and alignment) is the single biggest driver of senior marketers' business impact with a huge relative contribution of 20 percent.

And how about career success? Here, getting the mix right was also a significant driver of senior marketers' career success (7 percent).

Building and aligning a properly skilled marketing team is less difficult than it sounds. But to do it well, you'll need to put in time and energy—even if this means spending less time trying to keep your own technical marketing skills and knowledge up to date.

Let's take a deeper look at how you can design a team with the right skill mix to tackle the big issue. And let's find out how you can align your team so you're all walking in the same direction.

Design the Right Skills Mix

Here comes a surprise: the senior marketers in our research didn't have much confidence in their own or their team's skills. Only 60 percent believed they had strong conceptual and creative skills. And when it came to analytical and executional skills like pricing, the proportion was even lower, 49 percent.

In short, many marketers don't think they and their teams have the right functional marketing skills.

Were our marketers too self-critical? Perhaps. But when we dug deeper, we did find some significant skill gaps that marketers should address. Interestingly, "digital skills" weren't at the top of the list.

To help understand the skills situation of contemporary marketers better, we did a detailed analysis. First, we estimated from our data the importance of different functional marketing skills for marketers' business impact. Then we plotted the degree to which the marketers in our study, along with their teams, possessed those skills.

What we found is striking.

Conceptual/creative skills, like brand positioning and marketing strategy, matter a lot for business success—and marketers are really strong at both these skills. Seventy-six percent of our senior marketers, for example, were confident they and their teams were masters of marketing strategy.

However, analytic/executional skills, like setting prices and developing new products, are *at least as important* as these creative/ conceptual skills. But just 40 percent of senior marketers claimed to be good at tactical pricing, for example. There's obviously a significant mismatch between the skills that matter and the skills marketers have, especially in these more analytical areas.

And how about social and digital media skills? Marketers don't rate their own ability to execute on those skills too highly. But these skills aren't (yet) critical for the business success of our marketers either.

You might say: well, in the future, digital skills will be more important. We agree. But compared to the pricing skills gap in Figure 7.1, the widely discussed digital skills gap may be overstated.

What do these insights mean for you as a leader? Don't take our numbers too literally. Your situation may be very different from that of most of the senior marketers in our research. For instance, if prices in your market are highly regulated, pricing may be less important and digital and data skills may indeed be the biggest gap in your team.

Figure 7.1 Which Functional Skills Matter for Business Success—
and How Marketers Are Doing

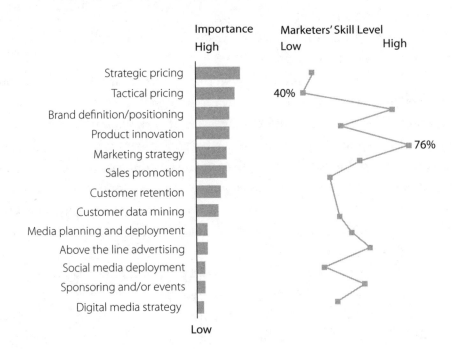

Importance of different functional skills as drivers of marketers' business impact. (One-
way between-subjects analysis of variance, p<0.01.)
Marketers' perception of own and team's skill levels, expressed as top-2 box percentage.

The Marketer's DNA-study, Barta and Barwise, 2016

The message is that you need to develop a team with *the right mix of
skills for what you are trying to achieve.* This sounds like an obvious, mother-
hood statement, but the evidence is that too few marketers are doing it.

Reviewing and adjusting the skills structure of your team to fit the
V-Zone issue can lead to breakthroughs in performance, as Christopher Macleod, marketing director of Transport for London (TfL), has
experienced.

When Christopher applied for the marketing director job, he
was of two minds. The job was important but came with a potentially

challenging task: revamping the marketing team at a complex and uncertain time.

The role as chief marketer for one of the world's busiest networks of trains, buses, and roads was exciting. TfL marketing is visible to millions of people every day, from the commuter to the prime minister. What's more, the city's most important event in decades was just around the corner—the 2012 Olympics. The marketing director would be tasked with getting the messages right for the masses of commuters and visitors, so the Games would run smoothly.

But TfL's marketing needed a shake-up. There were siloed marketing groups in the different parts of the business. Quality of execution was generally high but often not as integrated as it could be. It was the wrong team for the V-Zone. TfL's top marketer job included another tough task: cutting marketing costs by 20 percent.

When Christopher got the job, building the right team was his first big task. He wanted to know what skills the team had, where tasks overlapped, and which skills they were missing. He recalls, "It was difficult. We needed the rightly skilled team for the job. But we also needed it all up and running ahead of the Olympics." As part of a wider, pan-TfL review, he ran a series of workshops and benchmarking exercises to identify the critical tasks and optimum structure for marketing.

The review was followed by some long nights, where Christopher drew up TfL marketing's new shape: a unified team that would create consistent, high-quality marketing across the network to expand the V-Zone.

Once the plan was agreed, including buy-in from unions, speed mattered. Within days, Christopher announced the team changes and dozens of discussions and interviews for new roles got under way. Fortunately, they could offer staff options like transfers and voluntary redundancy. But the process was still painful for many.

As soon as the new team structure was set, Christopher's attention shifted to the team's morale and alignment. With the Olympics coming, he had to ensure everybody would be focused on the big task ahead. He walked the floors, talking about the importance of the new structure and the Olympics. "We have to be fit" was his analogy, explaining that TfL marketers, like the athletes, were now in the run-up to the big Games.

Christopher's work paid off. In staff surveys, the new team reported consistently improved scores for "collaboration," "doing better for customers," and "team supportiveness." Costs were reduced—with no loss in marketing effectiveness. And, for the Olympics marketing work, the team won two Golds in the IPA's* prestigious Marketing Effectiveness Awards.

"Restructuring the team ahead of the Olympics was like open heart surgery with the patient still working. But it was worth the risk. Getting the structure right was key," says Christopher.

Give your team's skills architecture your full focus. Accept that structure isn't a one-off project. Instead, your team's skills will need constant adjustment. People develop and move on. New skills gain relevance. Like Christopher, you're never done when it comes to designing your team. Successful marketing requires staying at the top of the skills league.

Recruit for Distinctiveness

Let's share an important approach that's helped many of our clients structure a team with the right skills mix: recruiting for distinctiveness. You can use this approach to review your existing team or as a guide for hiring new team members.

Marketers often tell us that it's hard to find the right team members. When we ask to see their team's job descriptions, they usually show us a needlessly complex document.

For example, one senior marketer showed us a list of what she wanted from a new team manager, including: *adaptability, business mindset, enthusiasm, entrepreneurship, emotional intelligence, willingness to learn, previous business-to-business marketing experience,* and *data mining.* When we challenged her list's length, she told us that what was most important to her was expertise in *data mining* and *entrepreneurship.* Most of

---

* Institute of Practitioners in Advertising. See www.warc.com.

the other things listed were standard competencies from the firm's HR framework. No wonder her team could never agree on a candidate!

When building a team, clarity matters. We recommend a brutally simple distinctiveness approach.

First, summarize your V-Zone challenge. For instance, your priority may be to increase margins by improving the retention and contribution of the most profitable customers, or to increase market share by better serving customer needs in a certain market. Whatever your V-Zone challenge is, clarity about it will greatly help you decide the right skills mix for the team.

Then, based on this, answer the following three questions:

- **Q1: What are the one or two most distinctive functional marketing skills needed to expand the V-Zone?**
  Don't write a long list of basic skills (most decent marketers will have those skills anyway). Focus only on distinctive skills—things your team or the individual must truly excel at. Make sure you've thought about both analytical and creative skills: most marketers focus on one of these, rather than both, reflecting their own personal preference and interest.
- **Q2: What are the one or two distinctive personality traits needed to expand the V-Zone?**
  For your team, which personality traits matter most? Do you especially need people who are entrepreneurial? Or people with a lot of stamina who'll never give up? Ideally, you'd have all of these, but which are the top one or two traits that will really make a difference?
- **Q3: Which personality traits are "no no's" for our team (fit)?**
  "Find people you like to hang out with," says Whole Foods CEO John Mackey. Look for people you like. But don't recruit too many people who are like you: that would reduce the team's diversity. You want people who are capable, committed, and good team players. You can afford a few difficult characters as "grit in the oyster" to challenge the majority's views. But they'd better be good and you

don't want too many of them. Define the few personality traits that are an absolute no no in your team.

The answers to these three questions should help you create a clear description of what you need for the team as a whole as well as for each individual contributor.

Once you've created a skills-and-traits sheet recording your answers to the three questions (Table 7.1), you'll be much clearer about what you're aiming for.

You can also use your list to take stock of your team's current mix of skills and traits. On a sheet of paper, next to each distinctive skill (and trait), write the names of team members with the particular skills and, if possible, whether their skill level is "world-class," "OK," or "weak." You'll soon see where you've got the right balance and where you need to invest.

Some people have suggested that our three-question approach is simplistic. Of course, other skills-and-traits assessments are more comprehensive. But in our experience, the longer your list, the harder it is to see the wood for the trees when you recruit. Less is more.

The three-question approach can also be used to complement a more sophisticated recruitment model. Take the example of a company that

Table 7.1 Distinctive Skills-and-Traits Sheet

The V-Zone Challenge _____

Distinctive Skills ①		Distinctive Traits ②
Analytic	Creative	

What's a "no-no" (fit)? ③

_____

_____

Barta and Barwise, 2016

has a validated model to predict marketing career success, based on a cognitive abilities test. That's great. You can use standardized tests like these to screen candidates first, while in interviews you look for the distinctive skills and traits you need in your team.

Before deciding on your final distinctive skills list, here are some additional considerations for getting the mix right.

Consider Networks and Networking Skills

A successful team often includes members who give the team access to important networks. For example, if product development is critical to expanding the V-Zone, you may hire someone with good contacts in the company's product development group, so bridging the silos is easier.

When building your team, think about the internal and external networks you need to access, and look for people who have the relevant contacts and skills.

Build Diverse Teams

Does the diversity of thinking, experience, and background matter for your marketing team? We believe it does. One recent global McKinsey study, for example, found that companies with diverse leadership create a 53 percent higher return on equity. Diverse teams will certainly enrich the ideas and energy of every marketing department.

Don't think just of the gender mix but also of nationality, age, religion, sexual orientation, previous experience, socioeconomic background, and ethnicity.

Clients sometimes ask, "How much diversity do we need?" There's no single answer. Specialist firms can help you decide on the right mix. But for starters, how about trying to mirror your customer base? That may not be 100 percent feasible, but moving in that direction could be a great start.

Decide: "Make or Buy?"

Marketing is changing fast. With digital, social, and mobile media and big data, most marketing teams are in the middle of a seemingly never-ending skills transformation.

Which skills do you need internally and which should you buy in? Two important factors can help you decide.

1. **A skill's strategic importance:** As a rule of thumb, if a skill can become a significant long-term competitive advantage, build it in-house. Procter & Gamble, for example, runs its own advertising effectiveness research, because it sees this as an important long-term competitive asset. Conversely, most telecom companies outsource advertising effectiveness research but invest heavily in in-house pricing capabilities because pricing is central to their business performance. If a skill could set you apart from competitors, don't outsource it—build it internally.

2. **A skill's timeliness:** Skills may take time to build internally. If you need a skill urgently, get going with external partners. If the skill is of strategic importance, make the building of internal capability an explicit part of these projects from the start (rather than waiting until the experts have left).

Build Marketing Leadership Skills

Most of what you'll read in this book isn't (yet) part of formal marketing training in organizations. That's starting to change as people realize that, to increase the company's V-Zone, creating long-term value for customers and the company, marketers need to improve their leadership skills. This doesn't just happen—it requires a conscious effort for marketers to learn to:

- Mobilize their boss (shape the agenda)
- Mobilize colleagues (. . . to serve customers better)
- Mobilize their teams (become a leader of leaders)
- Mobilize themselves (find purpose and inspire others)

When you are building your team's skills, think about marketing leadership skills too.

Establish a Structured Marketing Skills Training Path

Structured skills training during marketers' first two to five years should be a no-brainer. We are always surprised how many marketing teams don't have a skills development program.

If your team doesn't already have a structured skills training path, create one. At a minimum, it should incorporate different career points of generalists and specialists:

- Required functional marketing skills and training
- Required marketing leadership skills and training
- Required functional on-the-job experience

In the early stages of people's careers, much of the training will focus on functional marketing skills. But as people become more senior, you want the bulk of training to be about marketing leadership. Common topics are: agenda shaping, stepping up to mobilize colleagues, building highly effective marketing teams, and leading marketing with purpose.

Functional marketing skills training can often be done internally, combined with selected external skills workshops (e.g., run by agencies).

Marketing leadership training follows different rules. These are highly specialized courses, often tailored to your marketing team (remember: this isn't about generic leadership skills but about the particular skills people need in a marketing role). If you work for a small company, you may choose to send people to one of the few external marketing leadership training providers. But as soon as your team reaches ten or twelve members, tailored marketing leadership training is the better (and more cost-effective) option.

How many annual training days should you plan for? Here's an interesting insight: a recent study found that marketers are among the lowest spenders when it comes to training. Finance, HR, operations, and other functions are investing significantly more to "up" their people's skills. We recommend that every team member (including you) get at least five training days each year. Sounds like a lot? Well, that's about 2 percent of the staff's yearly work hours. And if this feels like a multiple of what you invest today, keep in mind that you are just catching up with your peers from other functions.

Skills development programs aren't only for big firms. If you have three marketers in a twelve-person company, there's nothing to stop you from writing a marketing skills development path on five sheets of paper. If in doubt, take two to three hours to write the plan together with your team.

Build Functional Skills Beyond Marketing

Marketing issues touch many departments. Marketers who've had exposure only within marketing will struggle to walk the talk and collaborate across the company. But most marketers haven't seen much of the world outside the marketing silo (74 percent of marketers in our study said they had only worked in marketing).

Try to rotate your people. Allow them to get three or six months' experience in, say, sales, finance, or operations.

For marketers, a stint in sales can prove especially valuable. PepsiCo, with iconic brands like Pepsi-Cola, Lay's, and Doritos, has started rotating sales and marketing leaders. "We have the belief . . . that what we need to build in the next generation of leaders coming up at PepsiCo is commercial acuity . . . we have started that journey and we have started with small steps. In some cases, moving people from big sales roles to big marketing roles, and the other way around," says former CMO Salman Amin.

A rotation will help your people build a better view of what's going on in other parts of the organization. It will also help to address the network point we made earlier.

Give Your Team Direction

Once you have the right people, the thing that becomes paramount is your team's alignment around the key priorities within the V-Zone.

Teams that don't focus on a jointly agreed priority are likely to get marginalized. Members of such teams complain that the organization isn't listening to them and that others call the shots. They and their leaders have limited influence.

Another symptom of a team lacking clear direction is that people don't prioritize their tasks well. Everyone's crazily busy and they say things like: "If only I had time to think about the bigger picture" (assuming they're even aware of the big picture). Instead of talking about the big issues for customers and the company, these teams are often tied up in internal projects and meetings that achieve little.

Thomas says: "In workshops, I sometimes ask members of a marketing team to write on a sheet of paper the answer to a simple question: Why do we, the marketing team, exist? Comparing the answers often stops the team leader in his or her tracks. Very rarely are the answers aligned. Typically, people have different views on what the marketing team is supposed to do, and that's often where the trouble starts."

But when teams have a clear, shared, energizing purpose, they can create remarkable results together. That's why successful marketing leaders spend so much time and effort aligning their teams behind a common purpose, as the example of Sholto Douglas-Home, CMO of the international recruitment firm, Hays, illustrates.

Early in his marketing career, Sholto experienced the power of team purpose in a way few other marketers have. This experience shaped how he went about building purpose in every marketing team he headed from then on.

For the new millennium, the British government decided to build the Millennium Experience, a complex and spectacular London exhibition celebrating human achievement. Twelve million visitors were expected.

Like many mega projects, the Millennium Experience started with much enthusiasm but was soon subjected to delays, financial crises, and public challenge, partly due to a lack of clarity about its aims and unhelpful meddling by politicians.

Sholto had the tricky role of leading the venture's marketing and communications team. As the project hit roadblocks, the team had to keep the many sponsors enthused while crafting the politically sensitive public communication under the critical eyes of government stakeholders. The pressure was relentless. But the team succeeded and was widely credited for the successful marketing of the mega project.*

"Everybody in the team wanted to make the Millennium Experience happen for our country. Our purpose kept us going even when things got tough," recalls Sholto.

Learning about the importance of a strong team purpose has served Sholto well in his later roles. At Hays, for example, he makes a continuous effort to align his team and other leaders behind the brand promise ("the right job can transform a person's life, the right person can transform a business"). The promise features in all key documents and is also discussed in important management meetings. After four years of sustained effort, 95 percent of Hays global staff now fully understand what the brand stands for in the marketplace—a new record.

But Sholto takes the alignment one level deeper. In a global organization with central and local marketing teams, he knows he can't simply align people behind one big marketing strategy. Of course, there is an overall global marketing strategy, but instead of interfering in regional marketing plans, Sholto established the wide use of a common marketing language ("awareness, acquisition, and engagement") to describe marketing strategies. Aligned marketing is a major contributor to the firm's profitable growth in a tough market.

Aligning your team is really important. And it's not a one-off activity. It takes relentless focus by you as the leader to ensure everyone in the team is chasing the same goal.

Seventy-three percent of all senior marketers in our study said they had aligned their team's structure and direction with the business. Our 360-degree boss and team data didn't have a directly comparable question. However, we found that only 46 percent of bosses and 45 percent of direct reports believed marketers emphasized the common corporate values to their teams.

---

*The operational delivery of the Millennium Experience was more mixed, but the Millennium Dome, built to house it, has been successfully reborn as the O2 Riverside Arena, a music and sports venue.

You may think you have aligned your team, but your boss and your team may not see it that way.

As a marketing leader, you're responsible for giving your team direction. They need to know where they're going, what their roles are, and how to focus their time and effort.

Giving direction requires you to be very clear about the big issue to be solved. Only then can you give strong direction to your team.

Here are some ways in which you can align your team.

Let Your Team Own the Big V-Zone Issue: Create a Marketing Team Mission

Getting your team to understand the V-Zone is just the beginning. To turn your vision into a reality, you also want them to engage emotionally and to start taking initiative.

Write the team mission together with your team. First, ask them to write answers to the question, Why do we exist as a team? The answers can be revealing, and will usually show that the team needs to align better.

Once you've discussed and clarified the big issue, step back and let the team shape its own mission. The resulting write-up should be very short (a couple of sentences is ideal) and will incorporate your vision for the brand and how the team wants to work together to achieve it.

Be creative and play around with wording and ideas, but make sure the final mission is crisp and memorable. For example:

> *Team Mission: Together we want to make xxx the most customer preferred (and bought) automotive parts brand while still generating a gross margin of at least 35 percent. We'll work together as one team, help each other out, and always raise issues that are in our way.*

Remind People Why the Team Exists. Repeat.

It's only human to forget things, especially given the pressure on marketers today. So make sure to keep reminding your team why it exists. At each team meeting, briefly reiterate the team's mission. This will take just a few seconds and you'll be surprised at how the constant repetition of a simple idea increases alignment.

Focus Your Team Externally

All marketing teams talk about customer focus, but all too often internal issues like budgets, project deadlines, and departmental relationships take over. You need to put explicit mechanisms in place to ensure an external focus.

One approach is to assign externally focused tasks to people on a regular basis (e.g., every one to three months), like conducting customer interviews or creating a competitor review. Also, after meetings, ask yourself: *How much did we talk about customers?*

You're the main agenda setter and role model, so make sure you talk more about customers than about internal issues.

Agree What *Not* to Do

Many marketing teams spend time on things that add little value. In the day-to-day workload, tasks that are "urgent but not important" tend to take priority. What's the cure?

Two or three times a year, hold a prioritization workshop to agree on what not to do.

Start with the team mission and ask, "What's on our plate right now?" "Which activities have the highest long-term value?" and "What should we stop doing, at least for now—or, perhaps, do only at a minimum 'satisficing' level."

Then lead a prioritization discussion to agree: key projects, projects to delegate and track, and projects to stop.

This workshop typically reduces wasted effort and improves team morale, as team members receive your explicit "permission" to prioritize the important over the urgent.

Critical Questions You Must Answer

Building a skilled team focused on the V-Zone is a big, big driver of senior marketers' business impact and, to a lesser extent, career success. Getting the team mix right means you must skillfully answer these questions:

Team Skills and Structure

- Does your team have the right mix of creative and analytical skills to enlarge the V-Zone?
- In recruiting people, especially leaders, do you consider their network and their networking skills?
- Are the people you're recruiting sufficiently diverse?
- Are you "building" and "buying" the right skills in the right order?
- To gain experience and expand networks, do you enable team members to rotate with other functions?
- Are you, the leader, building powerful marketing leadership skills too?
- Does your team have a proper skills development plan?

Team Direction

- Can the leaders on your team give a consistent answer to the question, "Why do we exist?"
- Do you often remind them why the team exists?
- Does your team have a mission that its leaders subscribe to wholeheartedly?
- Is your team's chief focus internal or external?
- Have you and your leaders agreed upon what "not to do" as a team?

You can also download these questions here:
www.marketingleader.org/download

| | | |

Cover Them in Trust

Your central question:

How do I get my team to ask, not for permission, but for forgiveness?

Think back to the best boss you've ever had. How did the quality of their leadership affect you? How much more productive were you? How much more did you enjoy your job?

The chances are that a great boss developed you by giving you tasks that stretched you enough, but didn't just throw you in the deep end without support. They delegated but were always there to help. Above all, they trusted you and had confidence in you—which, in turn, boosted your own confidence and gave you the scope to develop your skills.

When leading a team, never forget your experience as an underling who had to be managed by a team leader. There's a lot to be learned there.

Historically, bosses operated more through "command and control," telling people what to do, rewarding those who successfully followed instructions, and punishing those who didn't. Those days are largely gone. If your team isn't a great place for personal development, your best people will simply move on. You can't afford that.

The most successful marketing leaders build more than a team. They build a tribe—a close-knit group of capable, mutually supportive people who tackle the big issue together. Tribe members trust one another and have confidence in their own abilities.

Kristin Lemkau, CMO of JPMorgan Chase, summarized it this way: "As a tribe, you have each other's back and you're much more invested in [the] work ... [team members] feel their work is more meaningful; they understand the value of it."

Whether you're a brand manager, a marketing manager, or a CMO, aim to build a trusted and confident tribe.

Building a tribe accounted for 4 percent of senior marketers' business impact and 3 percent of their career success.

You may be thinking, *3 percent, 4 percent? That's less important than, say, functional skills.* In pure research terms, finding your team's best skills and traits mix (as discussed in the previous chapter) is certainly a bigger deal. True, but here's the thing: we only discuss statistically significant behaviors in this book. As we'll show you, building a trusted and confident tribe will make a perceptible difference to your impact.

Contribution to Marketers' Business Impact and Career Success

Business	Cover Them in Trust (4%)
Career	Cover Them in Trust (3%)

Variation in marketing leaders' perceived business impact and career success accounted for by this power as a percentage of the total variation accounted for by all 12 Powers in the neural network model (N = 1,232). In our research, what constitutes "Cover Them in Trust" is mainly the team leadership behaviors of delegating and collaborating.

The Marketer's DNA-study, Barta and Barwise, 2016

Seventy-eight percent of senior marketers in our research saw themselves as effective when it came to collaborating in teams. From a trust- and confidence-building perspective, that's good news.

But are marketers seen as great trust and confidence builders by others? To better understand this important question, we took a deep dive into our 360-degree data. We compared how marketers are seen by others through nineteen leadership behaviors related to "empowerment of people" and "team building." We found a number of very interesting things.

Bottom line, marketing leaders are seen as no better or worse trust and confidence builders than other leaders. Let's look at some of the different dimensions of what we found.

When it comes to minimizing secrecy within the organization, marketers tend to score higher than most other leaders. That's really good news, as this openness helps their teams build trust and identify issues faster.

At delegating, marketers are doing a pretty good job in the eyes of their direct reports. They involve direct reports in decision making, let people own their work stream, and tolerate the mistakes of people who take initiative.

But marketers' ability to delegate isn't so visible outside the marketing department. In fact, senior marketers' bosses and peers rated them below average at encouraging team members to make their own decisions.

The 360-degree view has also exposed two even larger opportunities for marketers: managing conflict and controlling their ego. (We don't mean you, of course.)

Senior marketers' direct reports, bosses, and peers all said marketers were less effective than other leaders at managing conflict in a way that strengthens the team. We know from our workshops that many marketers don't like conflict and sometimes find it hard to deal with difficult team dynamics.

To be fair, dealing with team conflict isn't pleasant. Yet good conflict management is essential for building a tribe. And learning conflict management skills can be very rewarding (we'll show you some techniques later in this chapter).

Direct reports, bosses, and peers also rated marketers below average at putting the interests of the group before their own personal goals. Some marketers have a reputation for inflated egos and selfishness. One marketing leader told us, "As a marketer, you grow up as an expert. You must prove your worth every day. Perhaps our ego is just used to wanting to look good?"

While some of the ego behaviors of marketers are understandable, putting your own interests before those of the group destroys trust. So keep your ego at bay. (Again, we'll discuss how later in this chapter.)

Building a confident and trusted tribe that takes initiative and owns the answers can be a big success driver for marketers, as Peter Markey, CMO of Britain's The Post Office, has learned.

Earlier in his career, Peter was a direct marketing manager at utility giant British Gas. Together with his team, Peter's job was to sell a wide range of services, from gas and electricity to household appliance insurance.

A passionate marketer, Peter was very involved in every aspect of his team's activities. He checked the mechanics of every campaign and made detailed suggestions for how they could be improved. Sometimes he would even finish off tasks his team had started, simply to move faster. Peter recalls, "I felt, as a strong leader, I had to be on top of everything."

The business was going well. But Peter and his team had to work harder to reach the increasingly high company targets. One year, it looked as if the team wouldn't make the numbers. Peter intervened even more. One evening, though, a young executive stopped Peter in his tracks, saying, "Your presence is killing my creativity. You are everywhere. You tell me exactly what do. You even do it for me. It's so frustrating." Peter was in shock. It had never occurred to him that his well-intentioned efforts would stifle the very people he wanted to help.

As a result of the conversation, Peter changed his strategy. He started giving people more room, asked for more ideas, and let them try things out. Soon, his new strategy paid big returns.

With the year-end nearing and the numbers still showing a gap, Peter asked his team to come up with additional revenue-enhancing ideas. In one session, a team member had a big idea: Why not start selling our products and services using outbound telemarketing rather than just traditional direct mail?

The team quickly ran a pilot and, based on its success, a new and highly cost-effective sales channel came on stream, which helped the team to hit its annual target.

Peter still remembers how giving people more space significantly increased performance and morale. His new style didn't just make him a better team leader. Delegating has become an accelerator for his blue chip career. Peter's mantra has become, "Let your team loose to be brilliant."

The best-performing marketing tribes have high trust and confidence among their members. These are factors that you, as the leader, have considerable power to influence. You can create a team culture within which people speak up, raise issues, make decisions, admit their weaknesses and work collaboratively, rather than as separate individuals.

You need a tribe of leaders that joins you in the battle to serve customers better and more profitably than competitors do. Only a confident team can do this.

Here are some ideas for how to build your tribe's trust and confidence. Many of these practices are valid for all teams—not just in marketing. We're sure they'll come in handy wherever your career path takes you.

Building Marketing Team Trust

Who do you trust? Why do you trust them?

In this book, we use a simple trust equation (you may have seen it before). It suggests that, to trust someone as a leader, you first need proof of their *professionalism* (expertise, reliability, etc.). But professionalism alone is not enough to build trust. You need to know a little more about that person as well (*intimacy*). Finally, you'd lose trust in that leader if they showed lots of *ego*. In other words, all the trust you build through your professionalism and intimacy gets divided by your ego. What remains is the trust you have available in any given relationship.

Trust Equation

$$\text{Trust} = \frac{\text{Professionalism} \times \text{Intimacy}}{\text{Ego}}$$

Sources: Maister, McKinsey & Company, Barta and Barwise

Team trust is key. You need it, so your team will dare to take risks. You also need trust because you want people to be candid.

Too often, people hide issues from their bosses, because they don't trust they can speak openly about problems and disagreements. That's a big issue in every organization, and even bigger in those with a "fear" culture. "The toughest thing in my role is that people don't dare to tell me things anymore," says Ford CMO Jim Farley. Conversely, Patrick recalls, "We once had a leader who told his team: 'I want you to bring me results, not problems.' We let him go, and everything improved."

You want people in your tribe to bring forward ideas and to take the initiative. But you also want them to reach out to you when they face issues to avoid nasty surprises and to help them find solutions as soon as possible.

In all organizations, people hide problems from their bosses *and* the bosses underestimate the extent to which that happens—despite doing exactly the same with their own bosses. In a good organization, that happens less, in a bad one, more.

It's vital to create a culture of trust and intimacy, where people feel able to reveal their weaknesses and problems. You need to work relentlessly to reinforce this, because a trust atmosphere doesn't develop naturally.

An open, trusting culture is completely consistent with a performance and accountability culture, discussed in the next chapter. But maintaining both—trust *plus* performance and accountability—requires constant effort.

Let's look at some practical ways to build trust within your team, focusing on the three elements in the trust equation.

Foster Professionalism in the Marketing Team

Obviously, you expect professionalism from every team member (and they expect it from you). Without professionalism, you'll never create a confident and successful team.

You're the role model. If you miss deadlines, so will your team. If you arrive late at meetings, so will your team. Whatever you do sets the tone for their behavior. So make sure you:

- **Keep your promises.** That, or don't make them. And apologize if you do fail to keep one.
- **Follow the rules.** Strictly and visibly adhere to company policies on expenses, confidentiality, equality, bullying and harassment, health and safety, and so on. You need to be pedantic and boring about this; lead from the front to create a zero-tolerance culture for lapses in professional standards.
- **Don't try or pretend to know everything about marketing.** This one is more challenging. The reality today is that many people on your team will (and should) know more than you do about the details of their work. The more senior you are, the more likely it is that some team members are doing things that didn't exist when you were their age and you don't understand in any detail today. So how can you maintain your authority and credibility if the team knows how much you don't know? Celebrate each team member's knowledge and expertise. You can also broaden their skills and link them to the bigger picture by asking open-ended questions like, "How can we do this even better?" "How does it complement other marketing activities—what's its particular contribution and what are its limitations?" and "What does this mean for the future of our business?" Don't hesitate to follow up by asking "Why?"—if they're on top of their area, they'll love to tell you more about how and why it contributes to tackling the big issue.

This may sound like pretty obvious, basic stuff. But you'd be surprised how many marketers struggle to be that consistently professional role model.

Our suggestion on professional behavior: just do it. No excuses.

Foster Intimacy

Can people on your team speak openly about their challenges and weaknesses? Can they easily ask for help?

Teams reaching this level of openness and intimacy are the most productive.

Teams find it hard to trust "perfect" people who stay closed and reveal little. In contrast, leaders who are willing to talk about their weaknesses and problems create intimacy and higher trust within the team. But talking about weaknesses isn't easy. What can you do about it?

- **At the most basic level, share small personal things within the team.** Take time to talk about family, hobbies, your last vacation, etc.
- **Ask for help.** Say things like: "Here's the plan, but the technical details about X aren't my strong suit, so Y, can you please lead on that?" Of course, one aim is to give Y a chance to shine, but another is to show how to present a gap in your knowledge without feeling embarrassed or defensive. Encourage other team members, especially the senior ones, to do the same.
- **Share what you're good at as well as what you're not good at.** Some leaders find it helpful to use personality tests like Myers-Briggs or the Five-Factor Model (often available for free) to get the discussion going. Sitting down with your team to discuss the results and what they mean for your day-to-day work can be very powerful. Michelle Peluso, CEO of online shopping site Gilt, gets her team to share their 360-degree assessments and talk about how they can help each other. Sharing assessments or organizing trust-building workshops with professional coaches are good ways of helping people better understand themselves and their colleagues.

Again: lead from the front. As the leader you must open up first. Once you reveal more about your own weaknesses, you give others license to do the same.

Fight Your Marketer's Ego

People pick up immediately on a leader's rampant ego. Ego is a trust killer. Thomas recalls, "I once had a marketing director who, on his first day, moved our team's fax machine into his office. He'd lost our trust before he'd even started."

Here are other examples that will show your tribe it's not all about you and your ego:

- Make your corner office a team room.
- Let other people present in important meetings, including to your boss.
- Back people up in a crisis.
- Stick to reasonable call times, especially for people in other time zones.
- When you receive praise about the team's work, pass it on to the team itself.

Great leaders make sure their teams can shine. When Tim Cook was giving the closing keynote at Apple's big product event in the Fall of 2015, he asked all the Apple team members in the hall to stand. In front of the large audience, and with millions of viewers online, Tim said it was a privilege to work with people who worked so hard making other's lives better. You can't put a value on that.

Build Marketing Team Confidence

Remember when you first learned to ride a bike? Perhaps you had someone who stood behind you, in case you fell, someone who gave you the confidence to try again until you could ride on your own.

"There's an inherent fear of failure, so you really have to motivate people to believe in themselves," says Ian Harebottle, CEO of mining company Gemfields. We couldn't summarize your role as confidence builder any better.

You're inspiring a marketing team to help the company increase the V-Zone. To succeed, people need the confidence to take risks. Many leaders overestimate their team members' confidence. Don't fall into this trap. If in doubt, assume there's lots of space to build more confidence in your marketing team.

As you go down the confidence-building route, stick to it consistently. And if you ever fail to do so (by challenging someone who took a reasonable initiative), make sure you apologize—you're also learning.

As a leader, building the confidence of your tribe is among the most rewarding things you can do. A great role model is Dawn Hudson, former president and CEO of Pepsi-Cola North America, who said in an interview, "I'd really rather be known for being a mentor and a leader—of men and women. Somebody who galvanized teams to achieve what they didn't think they could be doing."

Based on our experience over many years working with senior marketing teams, we'd like to suggest a number of confidence-building techniques for you.

Set a New Rule: "Ask for Forgiveness, Not Permission"

You need your team to act and take risks to drive the marketing agenda without always asking you for permission first. Sometimes they'll fail in a task or do things you don't like. You need to accept that. "Forgiveness, not permission" is a powerful rule, essential for creative marketing and innovation.

The alternative is a marketing team that lacks initiative, is only half engaged, and in which the best team members soon start looking for another job.

How can you put the "forgiveness, not permission" rule into practice? Tell your team you expect them to push ahead with projects and initiatives without always checking with you first, although you'll always be there for advice if they need it. You love updates, but you are OK if people make their own decisions and take measured risks to drive things forward.

If someone makes a mistake or steps on your (or someone else's) toes, accept their apology and explanation and, if at all possible, praise them for having taken the initiative. Find out what they've learned from the experience and make sure that this is shared with the team, so that everyone can benefit from it.

One or two people may get too gung ho, rushing ahead and taking unwarranted risks. You probably know who they are. Talk to them to make sure they don't do anything silly. But, most of the team won't be like that. Most are more likely to be too cautious because of a fear of failure. They'll need your encouragement to be more "pacey" and entrepreneurial.

Whenever someone takes a risk and succeeds—especially one of the more cautious team members—be sure to celebrate publicly!

Give a Word of Confidence in Every Marketing Meeting

How about starting meetings by telling your team how great they are and how you believe in their ability to deliver the company's mission? Or, when you close meetings, sharing your pride in the team members' abilities? These are simple things to do, but they can be big confidence builders. Try this for two weeks and see what happens.

Make Everybody's Voice Heard

There are many reasons why marketing team members don't speak up even in a high-trust environment: some may be introverts, some may be new, some junior, some not working in their first language.

You can't afford to miss the quieter team members' ideas. In marketing you are in the ideas business; you need the best ideas, whoever they come from.

Try insisting that each person in the room gives their opinion before you reach a decision. It's a great way to make speaking up routine, even for those who would otherwise hesitate.

Coach More, Tell Less

As a marketing leader under relentless time pressure, you might be tempted to give people answers rather than asking for suggestions. That's especially true when you're a successful marketer with more experience than most or all of the team. Even if you're right, that won't help your people grow, and it may demotivate them so much that they look for a job with a more encouraging boss.

To get started, try the 70/30/0 rule in meetings:

- **70 percent coaching ("you").** Turn 70 percent of your interactions with your team into coaching interventions. Help them develop their ideas by asking questions and encouraging further thinking. Supportive, open-ended "you questions" will encourage them to expand their ideas. Examples could be: "Building on your idea, how would you . . . ?" "Tell me more about what you mean by this." "How could you make this happen?"
- **30 percent ideas ("I").** Only 30 percent of your interaction should be your own ideas and proposals, ideally only after someone else has spoken.
- **0 percent of your interaction cuts people off ("I").** Don't worry about not making your point—the group will be aware that you have something to add, and they will usually give you the floor next. If you find yourself cutting someone off: pause, apologize, and encourage them to continue.

Switch from *I* to *you* more often. You'll be surprised at how many ideas exist in your team if you coach people—rather than telling them.

Teach Your Marketing Team How to Have a Good Fight

"How can I get my team to innovate more?" It's a common question clients ask. Constructive disagreement is part of the key.

Stanford professor Kathleen M. Eisenhardt and her colleagues observed top management team meetings in a dozen technology companies in Silicon Valley—obviously, an environment in which successful, customer-focused innovation is paramount. They found that the top teams in the most successful companies knew how to express their disagreements without falling out. Based mainly on her research, here are some ways to help you foster confidence and innovation in your marketing team.

- **Emphasize common goals.** Start your meetings by sharing the common goal: how you want to expand the V-Zone (for example, creating profitable growth or overtaking a dominant competitor). Refer back to the common goal when the discussion is going off-track or a fight erupts. End the meetings by reiterating how the team made progress toward the common goal.
- **Focus on current, factual data rather than opinions.** Discussions should be based on evidence, whenever possible. Conversely, gut feeling, expressed too quickly or passionately, can kill even the best ideas before they get a chance to live. At IBM, a team led by scientist Dharmendra Modha successfully created an innovative new microchip architecture inspired by the human brain. To innovate and collaborate better, the team used colors to label their arguments in emails (e.g., white for facts, green for ideas, and red for emotions). This shift forced everyone to stick to facts and ideas and avoid negative emotion (positive emotions were OK).
- **Explore several possible courses of action.** Don't narrow your team's options too fast; let them explore different routes and ideas to find the best way forward. This is hard, because you'll be operating under constant time pressure. But if it works in Silicon Valley. . . .
- **Create a balanced power structure.** Ensure that power, and airtime in meetings, is widely spread.
- **Genuinely listen.** People don't like autocratic bosses but they also don't like weak bosses who let the discussion go on and on or are influenced by offline lobbying. What they like and respect is a boss who ensures that everyone's voice is heard *and genuinely listened to* and who then reaches a decision (and explains the reasons) if a consensus doesn't emerge.

- **Help people think bigger.** Going further than genuinely listening: your people will grow and innovate when you ask questions to expand their frame of reference; not when you give them the answers. For your next project, try this: Tell your team that you want them to come up with the answers and that you'll only step in if needed. In meetings, don't give them your opinion; listen instead and try to expand people's ideas. Pose open-ended questions that start with, for example, "What if . . . ?" or "How would we . . . ?" for as long as you can. Step in with ideas only when the team gets stuck (but let them know that you are taking over only temporarily and why). Helping people think bigger instead of giving answers can be hard, but the effect can be amazing.
- **Use humor.** You set the tone. Humor can reduce the tension that results from disagreement. It can help a lot when things get difficult.

How confident is your team in its ability to innovate? Are team members willing and able to present creative, half-formed new ideas, or are they holding back? Do you often build on these ideas to improve them, or do you usually look for ways to shoot them down to keep the discussion on track? Whenever possible, are you sticking to facts in a discussion—or do you let hunches and emotions rule?

Part of creating an innovation culture is to teach the team the art of having a good fight. You are that teacher—lead from the front.

Call Out Deeper Interpersonal Conflicts

Despite your best efforts, there will sometimes be some interpersonal conflict within the marketing team. Left unaddressed, it can get worse over time. Initial symptoms can be small, such as two team members never sitting together and/or tending to cut each other off in discussions.

Trust your instincts. If you "feel" conflict, it's almost certainly there in reality.

Tackle it as soon as possible, typically through one-on-one discussions to find out what's driving the conflict, and work toward a resolution.

If it's proving too difficult for you to crack, don't let it drag on: bring in your HR experts or an external coach to resolve it before it starts to poison the team.

Find Ways to Create a "Good Enough" Relationship

If someone on your marketing team is really good, but you don't get along with him or her personally, aim for a relationship that's "good enough" instead of trying to move them off your team.

Sometimes people who think and act differently from how you and the majority do are exactly what you need. Chances are that, as a marketer, you are very sensitive to the quality of relationships. But if you aren't careful, your dislike of someone could easily lead to what INSEAD Professors Jean-François Manzoni and Jean-Louis Barsoux describe as the "set up to fail syndrome." Greatly simplified, it means the relationship spirals from bad to worse simply because—whatever the person does— you've already decided he or she isn't good.

Challenge your own assumptions: Why don't you like this person? Could he or she perform better if you did? Focus on his or her positive aspects, relax a bit, and things should improve. You don't have to go on vacation together.

You can sometimes build bridges by putting the team member on a project alongside another person you both get along with. This third person can become a link—or a buffer! If things get tricky, engage a coach. Even if you don't personally like someone, they may be an essential team asset. Building a "good enough" relationship and helping him or her be confident is worth the effort.

Be the Chief Mood Officer

Conducting an orchestra is an emotional, as well as a technical and artistic, process. If the conductor is nervous, the orchestra will be too. A confident conductor instead brings out the best from even the most difficult performers.

You're the conductor of your marketing team and all eyes will be on you. Part of your role as marketing leader is to be the chief mood officer.

Before each team interaction, ask yourself, *How do I want the team to feel?* Almost certainly, you'll want them to feel confident, appreciated, and optimistic. Lead from the front with the same confidence and optimism, and give plenty of praise and encouragement.

Be generous whenever it's justified, and when things are difficult, help the team manage negative emotions.

Critical Questions You Must Answer

High-performing marketing leaders build their tribes' trust and confidence. Ask yourself these questions:

Team Trust

- Are you leading from the front as a professional role model for your team? Are you punctual and reliable? Do you strictly follow the company's rules?
- Have you created a climate of intimacy in your team, so that people can openly talk about problems and issues?
- Do you manage your ego in a way that it doesn't erode trust?

Team Confidence

- Are you starting meetings with a word of confidence in your team?
- Do you ensure all voices in your team are heard?
- Are you telling more ("I") or coaching more ("you")?
- Is your team able to have constructive conflicts to produce better results?
- Do you call out deeper interpersonal team conflicts?
- Are you developing "good enough" relationships with people you don't like?
- Are you an effective chief mood officer for your team?

You can also download these questions here:
www.marketingleader.org/download

| | | |

Let the Outcomes Speak

Your central question:

How can I be a fair judge?

In the spirit of this chapter, let's start with the numbers.

In our research, aligning people's goals with the business objectives and holding them accountable for achieving these goals (Letting the Outcomes Speak) is a significant driver of senior marketers' business impact (6 percent relative contribution) and an even bigger deal for career success (9 percent relative contribution). To mobilize your team, managing performance is key.

But letting the outcomes speak is a major struggle for many marketers and one reason why many C-suite leaders don't trust them.

We'll now show you some numbers, which, if you are a marketing leader, don't read too nicely. But don't let these numbers pull you down:

Contribution to Marketers' Business Impact and Career Success

Business	Let the Outcomes Speak (6%)
Career	Let the Outcomes Speak (9%)

Variation in marketing leaders' perceived business impact and career success accounted for by this power as a percentage of the total variation accounted for by all 12 Powers in the neural network model (N = 1,232). In our research, what constitutes "Let the Outcomes Speak" is mainly the team leadership behaviors of aligning goals and incentives with business priorities and using merit as the criterion for performance management.

The Marketer's DNA-study, Barta and Barwise, 2016

we are confident every marketer can raise their performance management game, if they make the necessary effort.

Just 57 percent of all senior marketers in our research believed they were good at aligning team targets to business priorities. And only 63 percent thought they had built their teams based on merit.

So what's marketers' reputation as performance managers? Our 360-degree data had the answers, and the news isn't wonderful.

We first looked at how senior marketers' bosses and peers rated them along fifteen leadership behaviors under the headings "designing and aligning" (e.g., setting performance standards) and "rewarding and feedback" (e.g., fair compensation for impact). Across the board, the bosses and peers rated other functional leaders better than marketers at:

- Managing performance standards
- Enforcing the company's basic values
- Compensating people based on real performance

For example, only 54 percent of the bosses thought that marketers set high performance standards for their people (versus, for example, 60 percent for finance managers and 59 percent for sales managers). Not a huge difference, but not very impressive.

So marketers' bosses and peers think they aren't managing performance very well. What about their teams? You may have seen this one coming.

When we compared how the marketers' direct reports rated them with how other functional leaders' direct reports rated those leaders, a similar picture emerged: marketers' direct reports don't see marketers as great performance managers either. With regard to setting clear goals, compensating fairly, and putting in place the right systems for effective behavior, other leaders seem to do it better (see Figure 9.1).

"Letting the Outcomes Speak" is often the biggest challenge for many marketers, because it involves tough decisions. And being tough may be even harder in marketing where market outcomes almost always involve some element of luck.

Many CMOs have told us they don't want to be too hard on their people. That may be the wrong goal. As a leader, you are responsible for the team's performance. Most people are likely to thrive when they have

Figure 9.1 Marketers' Image versus the Image of Other Leaders, As Seen by Direct Reports

Difference in perception

The Marketer's DNA-study, Barta and Barwise, 2016

realistic stretch targets, when someone cares about their performance, and when results are rewarded fairly. Nick Reynolds, Lenovo's CMO for Asia-Pacific, calls his company's culture "performance driven" rather than "political," and Nick says he prefers it that way.

Given that many marketers find performance management tricky, we've made our list of suggestions a bit more comprehensive. We'll show you that performance management isn't rocket science but it does take focus, effort, and—most important—facts, in line with what Kathleen Eisenhardt observed in Silicon Valley. Consider the following examples of Alan Mulally and Luc Viardot.

The Power of Facts

Perhaps you remember CEO Alan Mulally, who was behind the Ford Motor Company's turnaround. When he took the helm at the near-bankrupt firm in 2006, he introduced what he called the Business Planning Review (BPR). Each week, the Ford business and functional leaders from around the world got together and reviewed where the company stood versus its list of financial targets and key initiatives. Mulally was of course the CEO but what he did, as we'll show you, holds valuable lessons for marketing leaders.

Naturally, there was initially a lot of pushback for Mulally's transparent and rigorous process. Some people disliked it and many initially hid the real numbers. But Mulally stood firm, threatening to fire those who declined to participate and publicly applauding people who shared issues and asked for help.

Mulally later recalled, "The BPR process is the foundation. It provides a fantastic window on the world—the whole team knows everything that is going on."

Changing a company's fortune through facts, numbers, and rigorous follow-up isn't just for CEOs like Mulally. Marketing leaders can do it too, as happened with Luc Viardot, a segment manager at Akzo Nobel.

When Luc joined the company as a product marketing manager in 2012, Akzo Nobel faced a serious business challenge. New regulation was on the horizon to suspend the substance Bisphenol A, widely used in aluminum and steel can coatings.

Akzo was one of the key players in this business. Its products were found in billions of cans of brands like Coca Cola, Pepsi-Cola, Nestlé, and many others. Scientific evidence about Bisphenol A's potential risk appeared patchy in 2012, and no company had yet fully qualified a replacement substance. When—despite controversy—a first ban was announced for cans manufactured and destined for the French market, it left Akzo and its competitors with the massive challenge to find a replacement by 2015—or lose the business.

Luc's first task was to help solve the Bisphenol A issue. Together with his team, he created full transparency about the status, success likelihood, and potential of each innovation project. Within weeks, Luc's data showed that most of the 200 existing projects for alternatives were dead ends. Through consistently presenting his analysis, Luc helped the Akzo leaders cull over 70 percent of all these projects and concentrate the resources on the most promising ones.

With this greater focus, the Akzo team found a Bisphenol A replacement in time, and was able to defend the business.

Luc recalls, "At first, nobody had transparency—we had to create it. Our data helped us convince the most skeptical people to focus all energy on projects with the highest success potential."

Luc has since applied his transparency approach to the ongoing business. His annual strategy process starts with extensive fact finding for each key market (e.g., customer developments), together with the global teams. Based on these facts, he creates the global strategy and then works with the country teams to shape consistent regional strategies, considering the unique needs of these markets.

Luc has also introduced bimonthly review meetings with all senior regional leaders to discuss progress (successes and issues) on the top priorities. To keep people focused, Luc and his team use only a few slides for the meeting, with green and red project traffic lights. The rigorous and fact-based marketing management is today a key success driver behind Akzo's strong business performance.

Marketers often tell us that they don't have the authority to run business reviews with the company's top management. Here's a secret: Luc didn't have this authority either. Instead he and his boss simply convinced other senior leaders of the need for bimonthly reviews, offering that the marketing department would prepare and lead them. And that's exactly what's happening.

Teams whose leaders know how to manage outcomes produce higher levels of performance. They're well focused and keep deadlines. Members don't use others' failures as an excuse for not delivering. People put in the required effort, because it leads to genuine appreciation, recognition, and praise from the leader and other team members. In a strong team, every team member is committed to the team's mission and reputation. These teams find it easier to attract and retain capable, ambitious people.

It's true: judging fairly can be uncomfortable at times. But it's key for your team's performance. And don't forget: creating a performance culture is a significant driver of marketing leaders' business impact and, especially, career success.

Here are some practical things you can do to be a better performance leader. P.S. We realize that many of the ideas on the following pages may seem like common knowledge. Trust us: in most marketing teams, they aren't common *practice*.

Build a Performance Culture

Set Targets and Deadlines for Every Task, Even Small Ones

Ambitious but realistic deadlines help people focus on what matters. They also energize people and create a sense of pace.

Try the following: from now on, always set a clear goal and a deadline for every task you agree upon as a team, even for small things. It will feel "over the top" at first, but widespread deadlines are the "perfume" that reminds people of the importance of performance.

Once performance has improved, you can relax a bit and focus goals and deadlines on critical tasks only.

Follow Up on Deadlines

Oddly enough, many marketing leaders set deadlines but don't follow through on them. The impact of forgotten deadlines on team performance is disastrous.

If following up isn't your strength, ask your assistant to keep a log of all agreed upon deadlines. Then, each morning, go over that day's deadlines and follow up with the appropriate parties.

Once deadline performance is good, you can go back to tracking only the most important tasks.

If a deadline is missed, following up is essential if you want to create a performance culture. Team members' confidence will also rise, because everyone knows what's expected of them.

Skip the Marketing Meeting Minutes
(As You Know Them)

Really? Here's a bold way to focus everybody's attention on action items from meetings without the typical meeting notes (which are often a pain to write and are delivered so far after the fact that they go unread):

- During each meeting, have one team member capture the most important agreements, including names, targets, and deadlines (but not who said what or why a decision was made).
- At the end of the meeting, ask the note-taker to read the to-do list aloud. During the reading, expect every attendee to capture his or her own to-do's.
- When you reconvene, have someone read out loud the to-do's again, so that each person is reminded of his or her obligations. This routine is very important! Team members are far more likely to remember and deliver on their to-do's if they know that the whole group is going to be reminded of everyone's particular tasks.

Try this for a few weeks. You'll be surprised how much clarity this simple approach creates and how much time it saves.

Reach Agreement with All Team Members on How They Spend Their Time

Formal job descriptions are essential, but most of what they say is forgotten once someone starts a job in marketing. They certainly aren't of much help in setting daily priorities.

In addition to the formal job description, we suggest that every three to six months you discuss two simple questions with each of your direct reports:

- **Question #1.** What's the most important thing you'll achieve over the next three to six months to help the team increase the V-Zone?
- **Question #2.** How (in broad percentages) will you allocate your time to achieve this goal?

Asking these two questions gets the team to focus on what matters most. It also helps members to push back if they're asked to work on something off-point.

Celebrate Success Often (Not Just Once a Year)

If athletes win a competition, they get medals and dowse one another with champagne. More important, these rewards take place in public. Do the equivalent for your team (perhaps without the champagne dowsing).

A culture that runs on performance celebrates success. Each week, there should be at least one thing you can celebrate, even if it involves no more than sending an encouraging email.

To ensure that these celebrations take place consistently, every Friday your assistant should ask you, "What successes have we celebrated this week?"

By actively recognizing and celebrating success, everyone gets to feel an uplifting and well-earned vibe on a regular basis. It then propels your marketing team to create more success, as they lean toward that feeling.

Hold People Accountable

Psychologist B. F. Skinner argued that behavior is shaped by its consequences. Skinner conducted experiments mostly with rats and pigeons. The same behavioral principle, however, applies in many contexts to human beings.

For instance, we've all seen parents who promise a reward to their children if they brush their teeth, sit still on a train, or whatever. Then, when the children scream and run around instead of doing what they're told, the parents back down and give the reward anyway, just to keep the children quiet. For the children, the thing being rewarded, of course, is their bad behavior.

Adults really aren't much different from children. We ignore the things we'd rather not do—when we feel that neglecting them has no consequence.

Let's look at this behavioral dynamic as it applies to marketing leaders and their teams.

As we've said, many marketing leaders find it emotionally hard to hold their team members accountable. Examples include: ignoring it when someone overspends a budget; letting project deadlines slip without properly digging into the reasons; accepting every possible excuse for failure to deliver a campaign; or setting targets without properly following them up.

In doing so, the leader dodges bad feelings temporarily, but nasty unintended consequences eventually materialize. The poor performers don't improve, and, even worse, the performers who do deliver feel undervalued and resentful.

In these situations, marketing leaders need to reassess their responsibilities. Being transparent about performance doesn't mean you don't care about people. As JPMorganChase's CMO, Kristin Lemkau, put it: "People just want to know that you care about them, and part of caring about them is being honest with them or telling it to them straight when they're struggling and even if they're not making it in a role. If they know you care about them, you can be nice *and* tough."

As the tribe leader, people expect you to be fair, transparent, and consistent. And while you can be supportive, you still have to judge performance.

Here are some approaches to help you hold people accountable.

Assess Your People (No Excuse)

In principle, everyone gets at least one annual review with two or three brief checkpoint reviews in between. In practice, though, these reviews often don't happen; at least, they don't happen in a timely fashion.

An erratic schedule leaves people without feedback on how they're performing and what needs to improve—and, even worse, makes them feel undervalued.

Regular evaluation isn't HR's job . . . it's yours.

Use Facts and Tangible Results to Assess Performance

It's hard to evaluate people against nebulous goals such as, "We need to strengthen our brand" or "Let's build up our customer-retention capabilities."

Targets in a marketing team must, wherever possible, be related to the big V-Zone issue you're tackling. They should be objective and, ideally, quantitative. Typical examples are volume market share, relative price, brand preference, annual customer retention percentage, and project delivery on time and on budget.

Leaders often tell us that marketing targets are hard to quantify. But when we work with their teams, we find that most work, no matter what it is, can be productively measured.

The only proviso is that measures sometimes need a qualitative dimension. For instance, if the target is to "increase the revenue of Product X by Y percent," you may also specify that this has to be achieved without a price increase or value-destroying promotion.

In a well-functioning team with common values, this qualitative dimension should be obvious and can remain unstated. But if your team is new, you may need to spell out the qualitative aspects in addition to the quantitative targets.

Also, where possible, the metrics should aim to take account of external conditions. For instance, market share may be a better measure than sales volume.

Setting quantitative targets takes more effort upfront, but it creates clarity and makes evaluation easier. As a rule of thumb in marketing, at least 50 percent of your people's targets should be quantitative.

Consider Having Others Evaluate Your People

A big issue in evaluations is *you*. In reviewing your direct reports, you can't be completely neutral. No way. Since you are leading them, every time you appraise a subordinate you're also judging yourself.

To combat that, we've helped several marketing leaders find a better approach.

In this model, a marketing leader works with peers from other departments to evaluate one another's teams. For example, you review the finance team, the IT leader reviews your team, and the finance leader reviews the IT team.

How does this work in practice?

Suppose you, as marketing leader, have agreed to evaluate a team member in finance.

First, you speak with the team member directly. You ask him or her about goals and how the year went.

Second, you talk with his or her boss, some coworkers, and a few direct reports, to get a relatively encompassing view of his or her performance. To add further objectivity, you may also look at the 360-degree data (if it's available). At the end, you'll have a pretty good, evidenced-based perspective on how this employee is doing.

Third, you meet again with your departmental peers (plus a representative from HR) who have evaluated your team and agree on the employee's performance and proposed ratings.

This I'll-review-yours-if-you-review-mine approach has several benefits. The evaluation becomes more objective and rigorous. It brings you face to face with performance issues in your team that you may not have seen or addressed. You also get to know how your nonmarketing peers lead and assess their teams.

Swapping evaluators takes a bit more time than the traditional "keeping it in the family"—but teams who've tried it don't want to switch back.

One client told us: "Initially, I thought the evaluator idea was crazy. It would take too much time. I'm now completely convinced. The new way is fairer and we learn more. I never want to go back to keeping it in the family."

Create a Development Map

Working for an organization, have you ever felt as if no one was looking after your career? This feeling, which can be traced back to the action or lack of action from the leaders above you, seems especially prevalent in marketing.

We recently spoke to a chief HR officer who even told us, "We don't do career planning. It only raises aspirations." We strongly disagree with this thinking. First, we think it's usually good to raise people's aspirations provided they're still realistic for the individual—and if they're unrealistic, the remedy is proper feedback. Second, for high-potential marketers, if you don't help them manage their careers within your company, there's a good chance that they'll take charge of their own destiny and go somewhere else.

Managing career plans isn't rocket science. Draw a career map for your team with an HR adviser. In practical terms, this means sitting down once or twice a year with your HR colleague and discussing your direct reports' career progress, expectations, and possible next moves (without them being present). Ask your direct reports to do the same with their team members and to share the results with you for reasons of talent development, succession planning, and anticipating gaps and problems before they arise.

A career map discussion gives everyone a good overview and allows you to speak with team members openly.

Everyone knows that marketing talent management will never be "perfect" in any organization. But a career map will be a big step forward for the entire team.

Find Ways to Reward Real Success (Not Just Effort)

For most marketers, success-based rewards are surprisingly rare. Many marketers tell us that their annual bonus has little to do with their achievements as an individual.

We understand that changing a bonus structure is complex. Such structures are often based on company-wide decisions.

That's why, as the team leader, you have to step up and act as a champion for your team. That requires two things:

1. You have to make a case for performance-based rewards to your boss.
2. You have to have data about your team's achievements, so you can back up your claims.

As a great tribe leader, you have to try—as hard as you can—to reward team members for their unique impact.

Be Ready to Bite the Bullet

As a marketing leader, you'll sometimes have to fire people. Unless you're a psychopath, you won't enjoy it, especially if you personally like the individual. But it's part of the job.

In some cases, the biggest mistake is not to bite the bullet. Jessica was head of marketing at a major nonprofit organization.* Her biggest team challenge was Ken. Jessica had hired Ken a year ago, but, despite all her coaching, he wasn't delivering on projects and showed little enthusiasm. Deep down, Jessica was pretty sure that he wouldn't turn the corner, but what if she was wrong? What if she had overlooked something? She

---

* Names and context have been changed.

decided to give it another try. In a meeting with HR they agreed that Ken would have three months to show what he was capable of. They set up weekly coaching meetings where he could discuss issues and receive help.

The arrangement with Ken looked promising. Unfortunately, it didn't work out. Ken came late to most of the coaching meetings. Jessica once overheard him in the hallway complaining about the organization. His performance didn't improve and was poisoning the atmosphere for the entire team. She couldn't let it continue.

Jessica called a meeting with Ken and HR, took a deep breath, and said, "Ken, I'm afraid it's bad news." (Incidentally, nice people don't like firing someone and tend to beat around the bush at the start of the meeting. It's actually kinder to do what Jessica did, telling Ken right away that it's bad news. They'll probably know anyway as soon as they enter the room, if not before, and it's best not to prolong the agony.) "This meeting is about your termination," Jessica continued, "I'm sorry. We'll do all we can to make this a smooth transition." Ken didn't look all that surprised. He said he felt that the nonprofit was the wrong place for him and moving on would be best for him too.

Ken's departure was a huge relief to the team. Jessica could feel the change immediately. In turn, the team realized that, while there was understanding and support, accountability mattered. Next time, she'd bite the bullet a bit sooner.

If someone isn't performing well, as a first step, always try to uncover the reasons why his or her performance is poor. Perhaps the individual needs help, is in the wrong role, or has personal problems. With coaching and support, he or she may be able to turn things around.

If this isn't working, give the employee a clear warning with measurable targets for improvement. If your efforts to "up" his or her level of performance still don't work, you should be rigorous in questioning whether you've done all you can and whether he or she might be better suited to a different role.

After that, if things still don't improve, work closely with HR and let the person go.

Critical Questions You Must Answer

As a marketing leader, assuming the role of team judge, who lets the outcomes speak and who holds people accountable, may not always be comfortable. But if you seriously want to increase your company's V-Zone—the overlap between customer and company needs—you must also keep and check performance standards. Creating a performance culture and enforcing accountability matters a lot for the growth of your leaders—and for your own impact and success. Think about these questions:

Team Performance

- Are you consistently setting task deadlines?
- Do you consistently follow up on deadlines?
- Do you record and follow up on actions agreed to at meetings, rather than just keeping "meeting minutes"?
- Have you agreed how your direct reports will roughly allocate their time?
- Do you celebrate team successes frequently and publicly?

Team Accountability

- Do you assess your team regularly without exception?
- Are your team's performance assessments based on facts and results?
- Are leaders from other departments helping you with your team assessment, so the judgments are more objective?
- Have you created a team development map that's regularly reviewed?
- Are your team's rewards directly linked to success and failure?
- If a team member persistently fails to perform, will you bite the bullet and, if necessary, let him or her go?

You can also download these questions here:
www.marketingleader.org/download

■ ■ ■

We've spent the better part of this book showing you how to expand the V-Zone by mobilizing your boss, your colleagues, and now your team. For you, this will be hard yet exciting work. Where will you find the energy needed to inspire others?

Let's take a look at how you can mobilize a particularly important individual: yourself.

SECTION IV MOBILIZE YOURSELF

"DREAMING, AFTER ALL,
IS A FORM OF PLANNING"

—GLORIA STEINEM

| | | |

Fall in Love with Your World

Your central question:

How can I inspire others with my expertise?

We've emphasized helping the company expand the overlap between customer needs and the company's own needs (the V-Zone) by mobilizing your boss, colleagues, and team. Expanding that Zone, however, can take time and relentless energy. You'll only be able to mobilize for the long term if you enjoy what you do—and if others can see your passion.

As a marketing leader, you're in the inspiration business. Think about it. Your boss can say no to your ideas. Your colleagues can choose to ignore your opinion. Even your team can vote with their feet if they don't agree with your direction (e.g., work half-heartedly or even leave the company).

Inspiration is simply an important part of marketing leadership.

But how does one inspire? It's actually straightforward: to inspire others, you've got to be inspired yourself. It's that simple.

Try this: think about a topic you don't care much about—something boring at work, doing your tax return, whatever isn't your thing. Then, stand before a mirror. Imagine that your reflection is a colleague. For thirty seconds, talk to your colleague about that boring topic. Look closely at the reflected face as you speak. What do you see?

Next, think of a topic you genuinely care about, something that excites you, something you really like. Again, for thirty seconds talk to your mirror colleague, but this time talk about that cared-for topic. See a difference? We're certain that your face will show more excitement. That liveliness behind your eyes is the flicker of inspiration. If you show others that flicker which lives behind your eyes, they'll be inspired, too.

Inspiration is easy to spot and tough to fake. Body language and facial expressions are so subtle and complex that even the most powerful computers can't fully simulate them (yet). That's why replacing humans in movies with digital look-alikes still doesn't work. The flicker isn't real.

The key to inspiring others is through your own inspiration. There's no shortcut.

In this and the following two chapters, we'll talk about three possible inspiration sources for you, starting with knowledge (customers, products, markets). We'll then cover your personal preferences ("what makes you tick"), and conclude with your vision. All three—knowledge, preferences, and vision—can be powerful sources of inspiration for you. And inspiration, as we'll demonstrate, is your biggest personal weapon as a marketing leader.

A Powerful Inspiration Source: Knowledge

For you as a marketing leader, what does knowledge mean and why would it inspire you?

Knowing the "what," "why," and "how" of your customers, your market, and your products is your lifeblood. It's why you get up in the morning.

Contribution to Marketers' Business Impact and Career Success

Business	Fall in Love with Your World (18%)
Career	Fall in Love with Your World (9%)

Variation in marketing leaders' perceived business impact and career success accounted for by this power as a percentage of the total variation accounted for by all 12 Powers in the neural network model (N = 1,232). In our research, what constitutes "Falling in Love with Your World" is mainly the knowledge about customers, the industry, and the company's products.

The Marketer's DNA-study, Barta and Barwise, 2016

To help your company expand the V-Zone, you must know what customers want, why they want it, and how they decide to buy. You must also understand what your competitors do, why they do what they do, and how they operate. And, to come up with innovative ways to market products, you need to know what those products are, why they exist, and enough about how they are being made.

This kind of detail inspires you. It allows you to excel. The more of it you know, the better able you are to do a great job.

Unsurprisingly, knowledge (we call it "Falling in Love with Your World") is extremely important for the marketing leaders in our study. It contributed 18 percent to business impact and 9 percent to career success. When you compare these numbers with the importance of other powers, you'll immediately see that for your success, knowledge is a big deal.

When we dug deeper into our data, we found a remarkable paradox: For your business impact, the key is having knowledge about your customers and markets. But what matters most for career success is knowing about your company's products.

Let's look at the expertise paradox in more detail.

As we said, for business impact, knowing customers and knowing the market are key, with "customer knowledge" alone receiving a weight of 9 percent and "market knowledge" 6 percent.

Contribution to Marketers' Business Impact and Career Success
("Fall in Love with Your World")

Business	Customer Knowledge (9%) Industry Knowledge (6%) Product Knowledge (2%)
Career	Customer Knowledge (1%) Industry Knowledge (3%) Product Knowledge (6%)

Variation in marketing leaders' perceived business impact and career success accounted for by these powers as a percentage of the total variation accounted for by all 12 Powers in the neural network model (N = 1,232). Differences versus cumulated results due to rounding.

The Marketer's DNA-study, Barta and Barwise, 2016

Conversely, when it comes to career success, it's all about your product knowledge. Strikingly, neither customer nor market knowledge was a strong driver of senior marketers' career success in our research. Product knowledge, though, showed up with a robust 6 percent relative contribution.

One might think that marketing leaders who know customers and the market get promoted more easily. Not true. To climb the organizational ladder, you must also speak your company's product language fluently.

As you might expect, of our senior marketers, 74 percent said they knew customers and 80 percent said they understood the market. That's good news (although we had hoped for numbers above 90 percent).

The proportion of senior marketers who believed they knew the company's products well was rather lower: 69 percent. For marketers to "up" their career prospects, this number should be higher.

But are marketers really known internally for their customer and market expertise? They aren't, and that's concerning. The Economist Intelligence Unit recently asked 389 senior executives a simple question, "Who is the voice of the customer in your company?" Only 32 percent listed their top marketer first.

Similarly, in our 360-degree study, only 65 percent of marketers' bosses said their marketers "ensure the marketing team recognizes the importance of knowing and meeting customers' requirements." This number puts marketers behind sales leaders (74 percent) and, perhaps surprisingly, general managers (70 percent).

As an inspiring marketing leader, you must become the most knowledgeable customer, market, and product expert in your company. Full stop.

To put it in the words of Wolfgang Baier, CEO of Singapore Post: "If you know your customers, everyone in the organization will want to engage with you."

If you are still looking for some ideas for how to build your knowledge, here are some practical suggestions.

Become a Customer Insider

When writing this book, we were torn: should we have a separate section on customer knowledge? After all, this is a book for marketers. Wouldn't telling marketers about the importance of knowing customers be like telling a fish about the importance of swimming?

Actually, no.

As we've seen, not every senior marketer knows customers well. Even the best companies lose touch with customers. When A. G. Lafley took the helm at P&G in 2000, for example, over 80 percent of the company's product launches were failing. A big part of his turnaround strategy was a program called "The consumer is the boss." It had a renewed emphasis on consumer insights—gathered from a wide range of research methods, including significant time spent by P&G managers talking directly to consumers.

Here are some ways for you to get closer to customers (in addition to the—still important—market research).

Don't Start in Marketing

A great way to gain deeper customer, market, and product knowledge is to begin a new job by spending time outside the marketing department. In other words, you start your introduction by getting to know some of your organization's other departments.

One marketing leader, let's call him David, told us how his new job in a US steel manufacturer took an unexpected turn when his boss, the COO, asked him not to join the marketing department right away.

The COO told David, "You know marketing, but you're completely new to steel. Unless you get up to speed on the technology basics, the products, the customers, and how the market works, no one will take you seriously. How will you know what's important?"

At first, the COO's counsel left David rattled. After all, he considered himself an excellent marketer. Finally, he agreed to a five-week introduction outside of marketing. It turned out to be one of his best career decisions.

Starting with the after-sales team, he learned that customers weren't delighted with the company's service performance. Everyone had a negative story to tell. "All the customers told me our company was big," said David, "but we weren't seen as the best. We were slow and dealing with us was complicated."

In sales, he saw that competition for large customers had become cutthroat, focused almost entirely on price. The sales team urgently needed new steel variants and better pricing options and techniques to keep competitors at bay. David discovered that the most profitable customers were midsize companies, who put more emphasis on quality, reliability, and service than on price. He also noticed that the sales and marketing departments didn't interact much—something he later changed.

For David, the week in the steel factories was the most humbling of all. He always thought of steel as a simple, basic commodity. Instead, he met some of the proudest engineers and shift leaders he'd ever come across and learned how complex and sophisticated steel production is.

In just five weeks, David learned about the pain points he could immediately address. He was still new to the steel business, but he now had an internal network and a much better grip on the big issues. Most important, he felt, people outside marketing respected him more than previous marketers, because he made the effort to understand the industry, the products, and other departments' issues.

David's advice: "If you can, always start outside of marketing."

Leave Your Desk

In principle, most marketers agree: some of the best business ideas come not from high-tech research, but from low-tech sources like talking and working with customers. Yet under today's relentless time pressures, it can be hard to get away from the office to spend quality time with customers, as Thomas has experienced firsthand: "When I recently introduced the idea of regular customer meetings to a group of bank executives, one replied, 'I'm already working twelve hours a day. When do you want me to have these meetings?' For decades, the bank has relied on customer research that was conducted by external experts. Subsequently, the bankers themselves had lost touch with their customers' lives.

The debate shifted when I asked each of these executives for a confidential estimate of how they spend their work hours, broken down into five categories: (1) driving the business, (2) productive meetings, (3) unproductive meetings, (4) internal emails, and (5) other. You could hear a pin drop when we showed the grouped results:

About 60 percent of their time fell into the productive categories 1 and 2. The rest was spent on largely unproductive activities. The group quickly agreed that they actually *could* make time for meeting customers."

A recent study found that just over half of employees' work hours in large US companies are spent on clearly productive activities: primary job duties (45 percent) and *useful* meetings (9 percent). The other half goes to emails (14 percent)—some useful, some not—interruptions and unproductive meetings (15 percent), administration (12 percent), and other tasks (5 percent).

"No time to meet customers" looks like a pretty weak excuse. Especially for you as a marketing leader. Time to get out of the office!

But how to talk with customers?

In B2B markets, talking with customers is simple. You ask them about their most important issues, their long-term plans, how you might be of help, and what your competitors are doing better than you. While they speak, you take notes. Afterward, you follow up.

In particular, aim to talk to two specific types of customer. First, the most innovative ones, because they can help you understand future market trends. Second, the most dissatisfied ones, because they can help you improve the customer experience, especially by addressing the main drivers of customer dissatisfaction that destroy customer loyalty.

Ideally, make an audio or video recording of your customers' comments. Verbatim comments and, especially, selected video clips can help you engage your bosses and colleagues with what's driving customer satisfaction and dissatisfaction. They're only anecdotal (and need to be followed up with systematic research to see how representative they are), but they're undeniable and emotionally engaging.

In B2C companies, watch focus group discussions from behind a mirror or sit in on depth interviews. Listen in to call center calls. Spend time in the field with sales people. Serve customers in stores.

Use your own and your competitors' products as often as possible under real-world market conditions and get your friends and family to do the same—and get as much feedback as you can.

If possible, watch how customers buy and use your products. Like CEOs Alan G. Lafley at P&G and Bart Becht at Reckitt Benckiser—push your team to do regular consumer home visits. Some of the ideas that emerged at P&G and Reckitt drove each company's success for many years.

How can you get at least half of your business ideas directly from customers?

Directly Ask Your Customers for Help

You can take the idea of observing customers a step further and ask them for help in developing your products.

Behind the success of the sportswear brand adidas are thousands of hours spent with consumers, jointly co-creating products and improving other aspects of the brand offering.

PepsiCo's former CMO Salman Amin reports some big successes from engaging consumers directly: "One example in the US is the Super Bowl work that Doritos has been doing for six years, which has been a fantastic experiment. We're inviting our consumers to come in and build advertising copy for a brand they love, and the response has been overwhelming. The other example is in the UK with the Walkers brand. We created a program called Do Us a Flavour, and more than a million flavor ideas came in from our consumers. And it's not so much because we wanted to get flavor ideas. It's more a way of engaging consumers such that they feel that they're part of the franchise and that we truly want to listen to them."

You don't need a big budget to co-develop with customers. We recently worked with a small food producer that, each week, invites five consumers for coffee and a chat. The company learns a lot from these customer discussions.

If you have more resources, you can scale up this approach using an online research panel. It's like having a bunch of customers in the next office. You can ask them questions any time you like with no lead time and usually get some answers within a few hours or even minutes.

Turn Research and Analytics Results into Insights

Do you *have* research—or do you *learn* from research?

Have you ever seen a company piling up tons of research reports without using them? It's a pretty common issue.

As an influential marketing leader, you must own your company's customer insights! Don't outsource or leave the gathering of insights to other departments.

In fact, owning the data isn't enough. You must ensure that your company gets world-class insights from its research.

Grab every opportunity to strengthen your company's collection, analysis, and use of customer data and insights. Better insights are often the key for improving and innovating around your offer, while keeping it customer relevant.

Ask yourself three questions:

1. Are we exploiting all the potential sources of customer insights—including, but not limited to, formal market research?
2. Are we using the data we have to develop actionable insights?
3. Are these insights reaching the key decision makers and are they then acting on them?

There's almost certainly room for improvement—quite likely on all three of these.

For example, on actionable insights, ask one of your team members to write a decision-focused one-page insight summary for each study. At its core should be three questions: 1. What's new? 2. Which insights can we use to change the business? and 3. What might be some practical implications?

If a particular strand of insights becomes too similar, repetitive, or hard to use, consider cutting this research and invest more in new sources of insight.

Remember, customer understanding is something that you, the marketing leader, must master better than anybody else in your company. It's the oxygen of customer-focused innovation, which is the main driver of long-term business performance.

Excursion: Getting Customer Insights from Big Data

Many marketers face a new challenge: how to get actionable customer insights from big data.

Because there's so much hype and confusion about big-data insights, here are some practical suggestions on approaching it.

"Big data" often means that there's lots of it, but also that most of it is generated as a byproduct of other things (e.g., the company's routine operations and consumers' social media conversations) rather than specifically for insight purposes. It's typically spread around the company and elsewhere in different formats and quite likely on incompatible legacy systems. It includes errors and missing values and isn't easy to analyze or distill. Basically, it's a mess. Relax. This is normal.

In a data-rich company, there may be several parallel big-data projects and you may be swamped with proposals for projects, approaches, and tools, most of which are almost impossible for non-specialists to evaluate. Again, chill. This, too, is normal.

Big data customer insights are primarily a leadership challenge, not a technical challenge. Your job as a marketing leader isn't to become a data expert, but to own the business thinking. See the big picture, ask the right questions, and only then bring in the experts. Here are some tips:

- **Step back. Ask yourself:** *What are the business issues we're tackling to expand the V-Zone?* There are endless things you could analyze—buzz, churn, distribution, feedback, comments on the competition, revenue, price trends, customer preferences, profitability, share of wallet, and so on. Don't try to include everything in your insight plan. Confirm which big issue you want to tackle for the business. Then, together with your team, set up hypotheses about which data might most help you expand the V-Zone for the business.
- **Create an information map of your company.** What customer-relevant information is flowing into and around the company today? Where? In what form? Few marketing departments have such a map, but it's a powerful way to find really good customer insights.
- **Pull out some data manually, and play with it.** However complex your systems are, you should be able to extract customer insights manually from a small sample of the relevant data. Do an initial,

(continued)

small-scale pilot analysis. By getting your hands dirty with this data, you'll start to develop an intuitive feel for what's there, how good it is, and the types of pattern and insight that might emerge from a full-scale analysis.

- **Get several views of potential full-scale data insights projects.** Invite, say, three firms to show you how they'd help generate insights that address your key business issues. Tell them what these issues are and brief them on what data you have and what you've found in your pilot analyses. Ask them what approach they'd use to generate and validate these types of insights routinely and at what scale in the future. Ask them about costs, timescales, and names of other companies who have used their recommended approach—and ask if you can talk to these other clients. Hearing several different views will give you a basis for comparison and greatly expand your understanding of what is and isn't possible and affordable.

- **Continue with manual insights analysis while you implement an IT solution.** A temptation with big data is to set up a big bells-and-whistles project that will supposedly get you amazing results . . . one day. This approach is typically expensive, inflexible, and slow, with a high failure rate. It may take a long time before you get any insights. Worse, you'll likely end up with the wrong design, especially if people have repeatedly tweaked it, adding even more complexity, as they think of more features that would be "nice to have." Instead, demand that every big-data project produces immediate insights at each step of the implementation—even if done manually along the way—so you can continuously learn and steer the project well.

- **Hire some good data analysts of your own.** This will enable you to use data analytics in parallel with more traditional sources of customer insights. Everyone else is looking for good data analysts so be prepared to pay a bit over the odds: this is a strategic investment. Every contemporary marketing team must have strong analytics capabilities.

Try to avoid running more than one or two significant data projects at the same time, and don't compromise on the steps above.

Become a Market Insider

It's obviously key to know customers well. But to become a successful marketing leader, as we have proven, you also need strong market knowledge. Market understanding is an issue that's often underappreciated by marketers. Don't be one of them! Here are some ideas for how to get up to speed on your industry.

Frequently Answer the Right Competitive Questions

If there isn't any regular competitive intelligence reporting in your company, set it up and drive it.

Here is a simple approach for how you can start with market insights. With your team, find out and discuss the answers to these four questions, briefly each quarter and more fully once a year:

1. How have our markets grown over time?
2. What are the long-term price and demand trends?
3. What are our main competitors' strategies?
4. What strategies would we deploy if we were them?

By your main competitors, we mean the small number whose actions will have the most impact on your success. Look at between two and five of these competitors—no more. Make it a combination of the biggest and the best or most dynamic. You might need to talk to your head of sales and the head of strategy, and maybe even your CEO, to decide which ones to focus on.

Read the top analysts' reports and financial press comments on your company and those of key competitors.

Some marketing leaders have even set aside half a day per quarter to role-play the main competitor—literally—to explore alternative strategies for them. We've also seen one team building a war room with charts on the walls, where the team paints the bigger picture of the evolution of the market and their main competitors. They role-play what these competitors might do next, taking account of the competitors' competitors—including their own company.

Provided you take the trouble to set up a competitive war game (get a bright graduate trainee to write a mini case study), you may be surprised how easy people find it to slip into the role of the CEO or CMO of a competitor. In fact, they'll often quite enjoy criticizing your own company and its strategy from the "outside"!

When understanding competitors, don't get submerged in detail: the aim is to understand the most important trends and get under your main competitors' skin to decide what their qualitative strategies are and incorporate them into your own strategy development.

Meet the Industry

"Going out and looking at our industry from a bird's-eye view allowed me to make some of the most far-reaching decisions for our business," says Roberto Berardi, marketing professor and a former president of Kimberly-Clark.

Aim to attend the top two to four industry conferences each year. Not many marketers do this—it can be highly revealing.

Step Back Regularly with Your Team

Sophie Cornish and Holly Tucker, founders of online marketplace notonthehighstreet.com, are known to take time out together every

January. They reflect on successes and competitive lessons learned, set their vision and direction for the coming year, and review their long-term plans.

You and your team should, similarly, take time out once a year to reflect on where you stand in the market and which competitive strategies will take you to the next S curve.

Each time we guide a team through such a strategic reflection process, the energy rises and, usually, more powerful ideas come out than people would have imagined.

Become a Product Insider

"The marketers I see failing are often the ones who don't understand the products and our portfolio well enough," says Michael Chivers, chief HR officer of global logistics company Maersk Line.

Lack of product knowledge is especially an issue for marketers who change industry. Banks and pharmaceutical companies, for example, often recruit consumer goods marketers, and the failure rate of these hires has been high. Knowing how to market soft drinks doesn't impress pharmaceutical executives enough to accept that your expertise transfers to their own sector.

As we have shown you, knowing your products well is a major career driver in marketing. Getting up to speed on the products should be a high priority for every marketing leader. Here are some ideas for how to do your homework.

Use Your Own Products (Whenever You Can)

One of the best ways to learn about your products is by being your own customer. Using your own products is easy when you work with consumer goods, like ice cream or T-shirts, although you need to allow for the fact that you may be unrepresentative of the wider market.

But what if your company makes products that you wouldn't typically use? It's a real challenge for many B2B marketing leaders. But even if you market products your team wouldn't normally use you can create usage opportunities. Matt Day, a former marketing director for Dulux, the international architectural paints brand, told us: "I had a young team, most of whom rented their homes on short leases and never painted. So I built in activities like renovating community facilities, using our color scheming services and products, on-site visits to trade customers, work-shadowing days with decorators, and regular trials in the R&D labs to test our products alongside competitors."

Work with the Product Development or Operations Teams

Spend time—days or even weeks—with the product or service design and development team. Building that relationship early on will show your respect for and interest in their work. You'll also get lots of insights into your new company's current and planned products before you set out to market them and, crucially, you'll get a feel for which potential future product changes or improvements would be easy or difficult to make.

Try to spend time with the product teams regularly. Some of these teams have weekly meetings. Ask if you can sit in on some. Or invite them to talk to your team about product development progress. You'll probably find that even very busy people will be glad to come to talk about what they're working on.

Some marketing leaders hold regular team meetings at a production site, using the opportunity for discussions with production (obviously, factories have strict productivity targets, so if you do this, ensure that you minimize disruption to the operation).

These meetings—even if short—can ground the team in the daily operational concerns. This will also help you understand, before deciding on a new initiative (e.g., a price promotion), which options will be easy to implement and which are likely to cause problems.

Getting close to the product development and operations teams can pay big dividends later, when you're working with the same people to improve the product or service at the heart of your customer offer.

Swap Team Members

Another way to increase your team's product understanding and their relationship with the product team is through team-member rotations (we covered this in the "Mobilize Your Team" section). In some companies, marketing and product teams exchange people for two or three months on a regular basis. Not only does this bring knowledge into the team. Strong networks with other departments also foster mutual respect, better communication, and the chance to benefit from new ideas and experiences.

Get Inside the Product P&L

As a marketing leader you must know what it really costs to make and deliver your product.

There are always variable costs and fixed costs. You need to understand these. Also, the way overheads are allocated always involves assumptions. Find out about these, so that you can question or review them if necessary.

For example, one client was about to drop an "unprofitable" product line when the CMO discovered that the line was being allocated an unfair proportion of fixed costs. In reality, the product line was quite profitable. It was only when the CMO challenged the product P&L that the decision to exit was revoked.

Make sure you have the P&Ls. Don't be satisfied until you've fully understood them. The bridges you should have already built with the finance team should come in handy here.

■   ■   ■

Knowledge can be a powerful inspiration source for you as a marketing leader. But sticking your neck out and gaining knowledge about the issues beyond pure marketing does way more for you: it can set you up for larger roles in the organization.

Michael M. Meier of search firm Egon Zehnder, a renowned CMO expert, shared this advice with us: "Especially in the early stages of your marketing career, don't narrow your interest down to just marketing. Instead, get a broader business perspective and gain experience in sales, trade marketing, and other commercial functions. That's what the most successful marketing leaders have done."

Critical Questions You Must Answer

Knowledge is a powerful source of inspiration for marketing leaders—and hence a key lever if you want to expand the V-Zone. Knowing customers and the industry contributes greatly to marketers' business impact. Conversely, product knowledge is an important driver of career success.

Customers
- How can you spend more time directly interacting with customers?
- Can you co-create with your customers in developing insights and better offers?
- How can you turn data into insights? Are you really getting value from your existing market research? Could you reallocate funds to create better insights?
- What's your strategy to generate and exploit big-data insights?

Market
- How can you run regular competitive assessments to understand the market dynamics and trends and competitors' strategies?
- Are you getting to the most important industry gatherings?
- Are you taking time out (maybe once a year) to reflect on where you stand versus the competition, and to adjust your plans?

Products
- Could you work more closely with the people who develop or produce your products and offers?
- How could you regularly swap team members with departments in charge of products and offers?
- Could you and your team find ways to spend more time on the shop floor?

- Do you have (and fully understand) your product P&L, the fixed and variable costs, and how overheads are allocated across different products and services?

You can also download these questions here:
www.marketingleader.org/download

| | | |

Know How
You Inspire

Your central question:

As a marketing leader, how can I leverage what makes me tick?

"Know Thyself"*

To repeat: as a marketing leader, you are in the inspiration business. Most of your role is to mobilize a wide range of other people to expand the company's V-Zone—the overlap between its customers' and its own needs.

Since you can't issue orders to your boss and colleagues, or even manage your team through "command and control," your best bet is to inspire them.

As we saw in the previous chapter, part of that inspiration will come from your knowledge of customers, the market, and products. Another

---

* Inscription in the forecourt of the ancient Greek Temple of Apollo at Delphi.

part of your inspiration will simply come from who you are and what you believe in.

Marketers sometimes ask us, How can I have more charisma? *Charisma*—the ability to inspire others—is often seen as a magical power that some people just have and others don't.

In reality, you don't need the grand ideas of a Henry Ford or a Mahatma Gandhi to inspire other people. Neither do you need the on-screen presence of a Marlon Brando or Laurence Olivier; or the rhetorical skills of a Cicero or Martin Luther King Jr. Inspiring others is much simpler than that—and you're already doing it.

In our marketing leadership workshops, people routinely discover that they already inspire others far more than they realize. And it's often the small things in their day-to-day behavior that inspire others most—behavior that they take for granted.

The workshops are intense. Participants work together for two to three days, developing influence strategies and building leadership skills. By the conclusion, they will have seen their peers repeatedly presenting, debating, and trying out new roles.

At the end of day two, we ask a simple question: Who in the room has inspired you? We hand everyone a stack of index cards and a pen and ask that they write about one inspirational person on each card. We also ask that they briefly write about why the person inspired them. We then collect all the cards and, late at night, slip each card under the hotel door of the inspiring person it mentions. Normally, 80 percent of the attendees receive at least one card.

The next day, as people enter the conference room, they'll find all the inspirational behaviors and traits written up on paper charts on the walls. You can hear a pin drop as people study the charts:

- "You have amazing energy."
- "You see business opportunities everywhere."
- "You stand up for what you believe."
- "You make me laugh, even when it's tough."
- "You're so committed to your team."
- "I love your passion for customers."

People soon realize that they already inspire others. And it's often small and simple actions that most inspire.

Our advice: find out how you inspire people today. Then double up on that inspirational behavior.

Before exploring deeper how you inspire, let's look at the facts from our study. Does knowing how you inspire others matter for success? It does!

In our research, self-awareness about their own inspirational qualities was a big driver of senior marketers' career success, with a relative contribution of 12 percent. Such self-awareness also reinforces their business impact, but the effect is only marginal with 2 percent relative contribution (but then, you'll only have business impact in the long run if you stick around).

Do marketers know how they inspire? We didn't ask them that question directly. Instead we wanted to know if they had the foundation for inspiration: awareness of their hopes, fears, strengths, and weaknesses. Most of our senior marketers (79 percent) said they knew themselves and their impact on others well. That's one of the highest scores in our study.

The bosses in our 360-degree database were (as usual) a bit more conservative. Only 66 percent stated that marketers made an effort to learn about themselves, and only 55 percent that marketers were good

Contribution to Marketers' Business Impact and Career Success

Business	Know How You Inspire (2%)
Career	Know How You Inspire (12%)

Variation in marketing leaders' perceived business impact and career success accounted for by this power as a percentage of the total variation accounted for by all 12 Powers in the neural network model (N = 1,232). In our research, what constitutes "Know How You Inspire" is mainly the leadership behaviors of learning about personal dreams, fears, strengths and weaknesses, and learning about the personal impact on others.

The Marketer's DNA-study, Barta and Barwise, 2016

at learning from mistakes. Nevertheless, these results still put marketers above average compared with how bosses saw their other direct reports (from finance, operations, etc.).

So, as a marketing leader, you should be pretty good at knowing yourself (even if your boss may think you aren't always learning from your mistakes). If you still need ideas, though, here are three useful steps to help you find and shape your inspirational core:

- **Step #1.** Confirm what makes you tick (the key step).
- **Step #2.** Find out how you inspire others today.
- **Step #3.** Develop your effective authenticity.

Step #1. Confirm What Makes You Tick

Why can't penguins fly? Because their bodies have evolved to be really good at something else: swimming underwater to catch fish.

Successful business leaders do what they're best at and find other people with complementary abilities to do the things they're less good at.

Sir Jonathan Ive, the brilliant lead designer at Apple behind its iconic iMac, iPhone, and iPad, wasn't a great—or happy—business leader at his design firm, Tangerine. His breakthrough came when he gave up being an independent entrepreneur and joined Apple to do what he does best and enjoys most: creating beautiful, functional, and intuitive products.

Chances are you too will find it easiest to be inspired if you're doing what you feel strongly about, believe in, enjoy, value, or simply desire dearly.

There's a helpful psychological metaphor: the Iceberg Model (see Figure 11.1). You may have seen it before. The point is simply that people's observable behaviors are the tip of a much larger iceberg of conscious and unconscious thoughts, feelings, assumptions, beliefs, values, and needs.

Becoming more aware of all of these unobservable things takes effort but is really important. The resulting insights will help you develop effective leadership strategies, especially ones that will enable you to inspire people.

Figure 11.1 Iceberg Model

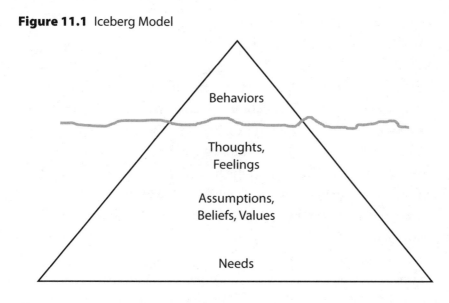

Behaviors

Thoughts,
Feelings

Assumptions,
Beliefs, Values

Needs

How can you get below the surface to understand what makes you tick? This is a crucial issue, so we'll dig into it in some detail.

First, widely available psychometric tests like Myers-Briggs, the Big Five, StrengthsFinder, or our own C-DNA customer leader tool are a good, quick way to uncover your general personality traits and preferences. If you've taken one or more of these tests in the past, we suggest you read your results again. Ask yourself: *What are the aspects of my personality that I find personally most defining or most important?*

Second, take a few minutes to reflect systematically on your career to date and your current job. We've found that answering three basic questions can help marketing leaders get a read on what inspires them professionally:

1. What drove the big decision(s) that got me to become a marketing leader?
2. What were the happiest moments in my career?
3. What most excites and engages me in my current role?

Third, to dig deeper into what makes you tick, we recommend a very effective exercise developed by leadership expert David Brown, called

"Why, why, why?" It'll take you about twenty to twenty-five minutes. If you do only one exercise in this chapter, do this one! You'll see why.

1. On separate sheets of paper, write six to ten roles you have in life (e.g., spouse, parent, friend, head of department, member of a management team, expert on a particular marketing discipline).
2. On each sheet, write down six to ten reasons why this role matters to you. Push yourself beyond the first couple that come to mind.
3. Take a look across all of your "whys" and pick three to five that show up on several sheets—even if you've used different words to describe them.

"Why, why, why" will tell you a lot about the things that really matter to you. And knowing what matters is a good starting point in building your inspiring leadership style.

Still looking for more insights into what makes you tick? Let's take our next lesson on what makes marketing leaders tick from Greek mythology.

Eros in a Logos World

Eros was the youngest of the ancient Greek gods on Mount Olympus. He had one irresistible skill: Eros could make someone love anyone he wished by wounding them with one of his arrows.

Eros's role and unique power made him a popular figure in Greek mythology. But with Eros's talent came problems. The other gods (mostly more rational "Logos" leaders) saw Eros as something of a wild boy. His acts were often seen as indiscriminate and inexplicable, with unpredictable and sometimes disastrous consequences. He showed no respect for age and status. That's why, despite his unique skills, the other gods never considered Eros sufficiently responsible to play a full part in the ruling Olympian family.

Sound familiar? Marketing leaders tend to have an Eros personality, but they work in companies dominated by Logos. And that creates an exciting tension.

Picture a typical company. Most of the leaders are concerned with Logos issues: processes, facts, and numbers. This makes sense. Managing production, finance, and IT, for example, requires precision and clear guidelines. A finance team's role is to understand and manage a firm's cash, costs, and investments in detail. CEOs have to deliver quarterly results, putting pressure on them to focus on the present and recent past in order to fix problems, drive performance, and keep the show on the road.

However, marketing leaders tend to be different from their Logos peers. Much like Eros, creating desire is what they love to do. A marketing leader's focus is much more on the future, the external market, and new ideas to increase the company's longer-term success.

Figure 11.2 How Senior Marketers See Themselves
Top and bottom two leadership behaviors, top-2 box, deviation from average, percentage points

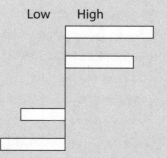

Open and creative (90%)

Big-picture thinker (85%)

...

Aligning goals/targets (57%)

Mobilizing role model (52%)

Barta and Barwise, 2016

As shown in Figure 11.2, of the senior marketers in our study, 90 percent described themselves as open and creative—the highest number across all the items we measured. Like Eros, marketers enjoy the emotional and outward-looking side of life, including making

(continued)

connections with other people. Eighty-five percent believed they were good at big-picture thinking.

Do their bosses agree? The picture couldn't be more cohesive! The superiors in our 360-degree database found marketers, compared to their other direct reports, to be more strategic and better at finding new business opportunities.

Bosses also recognized that marketers value personal connections. And they ranked marketers first, compared to all other leaders, when it came to exploring new ideas and learning opportunities.

In a boss's eyes, marketers are an enthusiastic, determined bunch with an outward-looking mindset. Marketers bring a unique Eros perspective to the business, including the ability to see opportunities and make connections.

However, marketers aren't so great at Logos skills—especially performance management. Just 57 percent said in our research they aligned their teams' targets and rewards around important business goals. Performance management, for many marketers, isn't a natural stronghold.

Unsurprisingly, in our 360-degree database, when it came to "making sure that performance standards are adhered to" bosses rated marketers lower than all their other direct reports.

The lack of Logos skills may explain why many marketers see themselves as outsiders in the organization. Only 52 percent believed they served as role models. Superiors agree that marketers don't always fit the norm. Just 48 percent of bosses believed marketers' "behavior is appropriate to a situation"—the lowest score among all their direct reports. Well, Eros wasn't seen as behaving appropriately either—in fact, he rather relished it when his actions wreaked havoc.

Marketers are often the Eros figures in a Logos world. They are passionate about customers, think strategically, and value connections. But they need to find ways to connect better with the many

(Logos) leaders who run today's organizations from an overwhelmingly rational perspective.

It's good to know where you stand on the Eros-Logos continuum.

If you are, for example, a rational Logos marketer, you may inspire people with your structure, clarity, facts, and figures. Clicking with other rational leaders, such as the CFO, will naturally be easier for you.

If you have more of an Eros personality, you'll perhaps inspire others mostly with your creativity, customer understanding, or ability to read people's needs.

Eros versus Logos—the question isn't "if" you inspire, but "how."

Find Out Where You Are on the Eros-Logos Scale

We developed a simplified Eros-Logos self-assessment tool based on our research. Do it now. Don't think too hard when you do this—just quickly tick what feels right. Then add up how many Eros words and how many Logos words you have ticked. This will give you a quick sense of roughly where you are on the spectrum.

Which describes your nature better?

Eros	Logos
Ideas	Facts
Strategy	Evidence
Imagination	Proof
Questions	Answers
Relationships	Power
Connecting people	Structuring issues
Mercy	Justice
Ambiguity is OK	Clarity is key

Look at your scores. Are you more Eros or Logos?

Step #2. Find Out How You Inspire Others Today

In our research, most marketing leaders scored relatively high on emotional intelligence and were already aware of what others thought of them. Still, if you'd like some other ways of understanding your impact on others, here are three powerful feedback methods you can use right away.

- **Feedback idea #1.** Ask five to ten people (friends and colleagues) how you inspire them. You want their honest opinions, so keep things as anonymous as you can. Perhaps use the index card method we discussed earlier.
- **Feedback idea #2.** Read through feedback that you received when you attended school or worked in other organizations. How have you inspired in the past?
- **Feedback idea #3.** Participate in a 360-degree assessment. A standard 360-degree survey will give you detailed quantitative feedback on your behaviors, strengths, and weaknesses. The best ones go even further, also incorporating forward-looking ideas and suggestions and giving people space to write about how you inspire them.

Step #3. Develop Your Effective Authenticity as a Marketing Leader

Inspiring others starts with knowing what you are best at. If you've done steps #1 and #2, chances are you know how you inspire.

The trick now is to take that knowledge and use it to develop effective authenticity. This means doubling up on how you inspire people most. And getting rid of self-destructive behaviors that may stand in your way.

Double Up on How You Inspire Most

Inspiring others isn't something you should leave to chance. It's a big part of your job. You must become systematic about inspiration.

Thomas recalls, "Some years ago I led a large global team, but despite major business success the team wasn't fired up. I soon realized that I needed to provide a spark. I was proud about the team's work, but I never told them. The team needed to see the flicker of my own inspiration, especially when projects got complex and overwhelming.

Soon I started each meeting by highlighting the importance of the team's work. When the meeting ended, I shared how proud I was about people's work and the progress the team had made.

Sharing how proud I was of the important work the team did was very inspiring for the team members. Doubling up on this inspiring behavior helped me build a very energized team."

How about reminding yourself of that, too? Perhaps you can make a small list of your most inspiring behaviors that you want to bring out more. Then set others alight by doubling up on these behaviors in each interaction you have.

Change (Or at Least Explain) Your Uninspiring Behaviors

There's a fine line between authenticity and *effective* authenticity.

Authentic leadership is a powerful concept that's often misunderstood. The core idea is that you build the legitimacy of your leadership on honest and ethical relationships, including by being honest about who you are rather than trying to be someone else.

Many people, however, translate this into "I'm great. I'll be most successful if I don't change." Well, that assumes that you're already an inspirational and effective leader. Perhaps you are, but you'd be an exception.

Unfortunately, most of us display—at times—destructive leadership behaviors. We show off, shout in front of others, make sarcastic comments, cut people off, and so on.

As you observe how your behavior impacts others, also take note of these negatives.

But how do you deal with those uninspiring characteristics that define you? What can you do about them?

First, try to stop these behaviors! Anything you can do to reduce your destructive actions will be helpful.

For instance, as chairman of Which?, the UK's leading consumer organization, Patrick learned: "When introducing an item at meetings, I also tended to provide the answer to the problem, as I saw it. My colleagues agreed that I was often—in fact, usually they said—right, but not always, and starting a discussion with what the chairman thinks is the answer isn't a great way to encourage fresh ideas and open debate. I learned, with some difficulty, to withhold my own views, at least until later in the discussion."

Behavior modification is difficult and usually takes time—especially when it's something you've been doing unconsciously for many years. Alternatively, try to explain your less-helpful behaviors in order to help those around you handle them better, as the following disguised example shows.

Craig* is a typical Eros marketing leader. A marketing manager at an Asian airline, he's passionate about customer service. For example, he looks after the company's customer satisfaction tracking and regularly speaks with customers. He once said, "I can feel if a service idea is good."

But not everybody got along well with Craig. His counterpart in finance, Andrea, a senior analyst, initially, found him impossible to work with.

Andrea knew that marketing is sometimes hard to measure, but she always felt that Craig's numbers were particularly weak, even sloppy.

One day Andrea and Craig clashed in a meeting. Craig was explaining his latest marketing returns report, when Andrea interrupted him, saying that she felt the numbers were a joke and that Craig made her feel that financial returns were irrelevant. In the coming weeks, they barely exchanged a word. Craig was angry, because, according to him, Andrea simply couldn't understand what it takes to delight customers. And Andrea thought Craig simply had his head in the clouds.

---

* Name and context have been changed.

It took the intervention of Craig's boss to get both in a room together to talk about what had happened. But instead of dwelling on the past, he asked each of them to talk about what he or she felt was most important for the future of the business. Andrea started with a passionate speech about improving the P&L to keep the company alive. Craig spoke with similar passion about why customer service was at the heart of all that mattered.

The discussion had a big effect on Craig and Andrea. They realized that both bring passion and very different skills to the table. What they found uninspiring in their counterpart was actually important for the company. Craig understood that Andrea's numbers focus was key for meeting their quarterly targets. Andrea recognized that Craig's customer service ideas were essential for the airline and sometimes simply hard to express in numbers. She would never have his ideas or his level of customer understanding.

Andrea recalls: "Craig became inspiring to me when he explained why he'll never be great at analytics, but why his creativity helps the company."

Explaining your behavior can be surprisingly powerful. Another CMO we work with told her team, "At times I'm impulsive. I don't mean it to frighten you. It's just how I am. But if I start going overboard, I may not realize it. Please tell me immediately."

Another leader explained to his colleagues that he's quite introverted. Even when he has ideas, he sometimes stays quiet, because fighting for airtime isn't natural for him.

If you have uninspiring behaviors that hamper your effectiveness as a leader, try to reduce or stop them. If that's too hard, help others get along with you by explaining your uninspiring behaviors and why you may struggle to eliminate them.

None of the many successful leaders we've worked with would say, "My natural style is the most effective." What they would say instead is along the lines of, "I've built on my most inspiring behaviors and done my best to change—or at least explain—things that stand in my way of being inspirational."

So when you develop your own effective marketing leadership style, consider doubling up on how you inspire others most, and change (or at least explain) your uninspiring behaviors.

That's effective authentic marketing leadership.

Critical Questions You Must Answer

As a marketing leader, knowing yourself and your impact on others is a big career driver and also reinforces your business impact. To expand your influence and your company's V-Zone, you must understand which aspects of your personality inspire other people, so you can mobilize them better.

Ask yourself:

- What makes you tick (in a way that inspires both you and others)? In particular:
- What drove the big decision(s) that got you to become a marketing leader?
- What were the happiest moments in your marketing career?
- What most excites and engages you in your current role?
- How might you inspire others today?
- How could you double up on the things you do that most inspire others?
- What negative behaviors should you try to stop, or at least explain to those around you?
- What's your most effective authentic marketing leadership style?

You can also download these questions here:
www.marketingleader.org/download

| | | |

Aim
Higher

Your central question:

What's your marketing leadership vision?

The Logo on Times Square

When Simon Kang took charge of LG's appliances business in the United States in early 2000, few people would have put money on his chances of success.

To start with, there was no real US business. Lucky Goldstar, the previous brand name, had been launched there with few products and a shoestring budget. Awareness of the new LG brand was minimal.

Simon's business background was mostly in finance. He hadn't done much marketing before, and he knew little about brand building. With little budget and support, the odds weren't in his favor.

Then one evening, while resting on the sofa after a long day in the office, Simon had a dream: "I want to see a neon sign with the LG logo on Times Square—next to the country's most prestigious brands."

For Simon, this ambitious vision helped inspire a series of creative, headline-grabbing product ideas and marketing stunts. Together with a marketing agency, he developed the concept of "intelligent ideas, delightful discoveries"—clever products that inspire people to discover new ways of using them.

Within a few months, he'd designed colored fridges, developed smart new product features, put up individual outdoor ads in front of dealers' stores (all LG could afford), and flown buyers over to Korea to see the R&D labs and meet the top management.

His big dream carried him through numerous meetings, where he convinced the LG board, his colleagues in the factories, and his own team to trust him and create the unusual products he wanted.

It worked. Today LG is a leading household brand in the United States.

And the LG sign in Times Square? Go take a look!

The Inspirational Power of Your Vision

Leading marketing is rewarding in many ways. But mobilizing your boss, your colleagues, and your team to expand the V-Zone will also involve long hours and high pressure. Often, you'll have to overcome barriers, manage conflicts, and take risks.

We've so far looked at two possible sources of inspiration that keep you going and help you inspire others: "falling in love with your world" (knowledge of customers, the market, and the company's products) and "know how you inspire" (what makes you tick).

As Simon's story has taught us, a big dream can help you achieve things you didn't deem possible—and inspire others. That's why we now discuss your third powerful source of inspiration: an ambitious, motivating *vision* of where you want to be.

"Aim Higher" is the last of the 12 Powers which—in combination—will enable you to mobilize your boss, your colleagues, your team, and yourself, increase your business impact and career success, and help the company maximize its V-Zone.

Let's take a closer look.

Do You Need "The Vision Thing"?

For decades, leadership books hammered home the idea that leaders should act with "the end in mind" (e.g., "What do you want people to say at your funeral?"). Many leaders indeed found developing a vision very powerful—Simon Kang surely did.

But not everyone is convinced. "Too much goal setting kills creativity" or "What happens, happens," are challenges we hear often as we present to marketers the idea of a personal leadership vision.

Our data shows: the marketing vision skeptics are wrong.

Having an inspiring personal vision (we call it Aim Higher) is a significant driver of marketers' business impact (5 percent relative contribution), and—together with Walk the Halls—the largest driver of their career success (13 percent relative contribution).

Do you, as a successful marketing leader, need an inspiring vision? You do!

Contribution to Marketers' Business Impact and Career Success

Business	Aim Higher (5%)
Career	Aim Higher (13%)

Variation in marketing leaders' perceived business impact and career success accounted for by this power as a percentage of the total variation accounted for by all 12 Powers in the neural network model (N = 1,232). In our research, what constitutes "Aim Higher" is mainly the personal vision for life, the business, and one's own career, as well as the discipline to follow through.

The Marketer's DNA-study, Barta and Barwise, 2016

When we spoke to successful marketing leaders for this book, almost all had ambitious, higher-order aims. One CMO, for example, wanted to help kids get better nutrition, and built a brand around that. Another was keen to bring better products to his home market, a developing country. We met a top marketer who wanted to make it to CEO soon, so that she could lead and coach larger teams. And one CMO, since he started out, simply always had the dream to become a CMO.

If you think about it, you'll immediately see why your personal vision is so critical. Expanding the V-Zone doesn't happen overnight. Upward, you must mobilize your boss to win top team support. Sideways, you and your team must mobilize people in other departments to ensure that the company consistently delivers the right customer experience. And below you, you need to mobilize your team to become the leaders you need to help solve the big company issues. It's a process that typically takes months or even years—if the CMO is given that long. You need to be really clear and convinced about where you want to go. An inspiring personal vision will make mobilizing others much easier for you.

Marketers score high when it comes to vision. Of the senior marketers in our research, 77 percent said they had a clear customer vision and even 81 percent said the same about their career vision. The number was lower for life priorities: 58 percent (life priorities are obviously a harder nut to crack for many of us).

Aiming higher isn't just about your brand or your business. We could see in our study: the most successful marketers align customer and company needs with their own career priorities and life priorities. Such an aligned vision will help you inspire other people and keep going when things get difficult.

However, when your personal and professional aims are fundamentally misaligned, you'll struggle to find the energy to make them happen.

Imagine, for example, you set high ambitions for your soft drinks brand, but your day job doesn't fit your career aims because what you really dream of is opening a surfing school. Or your career aim is, say, becoming a Fortune 500 CMO, but that clashes with your desire to have five kids and spend time with them each day. In situations like these, your plan may sooner or later fall apart. And that implosion can be very painful.

To be fair: integrating job and life priorities perfectly can be an illusion (as most parents will confirm). There will always be trade-offs. The best you can do is make an honest assessment of what you're striving for, aim high, and give it a shot. That said, so much clarity will already set you apart in the field.

This book specifically aims to help *marketers* become marketing leaders, so we won't go as deeply into your life priorities as most general leadership books do (some of the exercises in part of the book, such as "why, why, why?" will, however, give you a good steer on this).

Let's look at a simple way to help you craft your marketing leadership vision, so you can aim higher.

Write Your Marketing Leadership Manifesto

Many of the successful marketing leaders who helped us with this book have a written manifesto of some sort. The Marketing Society, in its manifesto for marketing leadership, recommends that marketers write down a vision for how to succeed, so they can inspire a customer-led organization and create customer value. We are convinced you too will benefit from having a written leadership manifesto. It's a powerful way to shape your goals with the right words that capture it and make it concrete.

Imagine, in a year from now you open a letter that you've written to yourself today, titled "My Marketing Leadership Manifesto." The letter is about the goals you set for your private life and for your professional life as a marketing leader. What would you write today?

The previous chapters should have given you lots of food for thought about what you want to achieve and what type of leader you want to be.

When you write your manifesto, don't just think about increasing the V-Zone. Also consider your career path and how your work ties in with your family life and overall aspirations.

It's time to get concrete and write your manifesto (if you haven't done this already). Find a place where you can be alone and undistracted for the next forty-five minutes. Then write your manifesto, considering: (1) Where do I want to be five years from now? (2) Which key steps will I take to get there?

Areas you could cover in your manifesto are, for example:

- The difference you will be making to customers and the industry
- The impact you will have had on the business—its culture and its performance
- Where you will stand in your career
- What difference do you want to make to people who matter to you?
- How happy and healthy will you be; how will you integrate work and your private life?

This is *your* manifesto—write it in any way you like. Use a story, free-form text, bullet points. It doesn't matter. The only thing that matters is for this manifesto to represent you.

Once you are done, share and discuss your manifesto with people you trust. It's often a great way to sharpen your ideas or to get additional insights and clarity.

Here are two example manifestos written by marketing leaders in our workshops.

- *I am making a big contribution to people through my marketing role. I have built XXX into the most desired brand for customers and I am now the CMO. As a board member, I have more influence over how we serve customers. I have built the best team in the industry. We are known as the place where people start and build great marketing careers. I always work with my husband to find ways to make my career happen, aiming for the best possible balance between my work and my family life.*
- *I'm ensuring (YYY) is the best choice for women in any age group, by giving them access to products based on the latest (ZZZZ) technologies. Through this I help them build confidence. I am now leading marketing across the entire (YYY) group to help it move*

its market position from second to first with my passion and ideas. People know me as the best talent builder in the company. Throughout my work, I aim to leverage my creative skills, but I'm also increasingly learning to be more analytical. I still work part-time. Working 4 days a week is hard, but it's the only way I can spend real quality time with my three kids. I've lost weight and I now fit into the red polo shirt again.

To inspire others, you first have to be inspired. There's no shortcut. Once you have an inspiring vision as a marketing leader, let it shine!

Critical Questions You Must Answer

A vision that connects your professional marketing goals with your personal goals will help you inspire and mobilize others, and through this, expand the V-Zone.

- What's your inspiring vision?
- What's your Marketing Leadership Manifesto?

You can also download these questions here:
www.marketingleader.org/download

It's Time for Your Launch

Becoming an influential marketing leader is among the most exciting professional ventures in many ways. By increasing your influence, you'll help the company expand its V-Zone and, therefore, its long-term business performance. At a personal level, you'll also increase both your business impact and your career success.

Mastering the 12 Powers of a marketing leader will help you gain more traction by mobilizing the key people around you: your boss, your nonmarketing colleagues, and your team. But most important, the 12 Powers will help you to mobilize yourself to have the energy and inspiration to achieve what distinctive marketing leaders achieve: expand the V-Zone.

Luckily, you don't have to be born as a marketing leader. As our research bears out, you can learn the critical leadership behaviors for success in marketing.

You've gotten to where you are because of what you're good at. Build on that—don't try to change everything. Instead, at least for now, work on just a few of the areas we've covered—ideally, those that will give you the biggest bang for the buck.

Don't try too much too fast. Go for smaller changes—but give them attention.

Look back through the book and list the ideas you find most powerful. Then ask yourself, *Which of the leadership behaviors I listed will have the biggest impact on my effectiveness and success as a marketing leader? Which behaviors can I realistically implement in the next six to twelve months?*

Pick a maximum of three—your *Big Three.* Think of these as the three mission critical leadership efforts you'll make, even when things get tough.

Be specific and add a deadline wherever you can (without the rigidity of a Soviet-era five-year plan).

My Big Three

1.

2.

3.

Once you're happy, share your list with a friend or mentor. Ask him or her to challenge you: "Are these the most effective changes I can make now? Can I chew them off?" Ask the person to follow up with you from time to time on how you're doing.

What If the CEO Doesn't Get It?

The 12 Powers discussed here account for most of the explicable variation in marketers' effectiveness and success. But organizational issues (e.g., having enough resources and a clear, consistent, and accountable role) will also significantly affect your business impact and, especially, career success. Ultimately, these are down to the CEO. What if, despite your best attempts, the CEO and the rest of the top team still don't get it? What if they talk the talk but don't support your efforts to expand the V-Zone and build long-term value for the customers and the company? Start looking for another job! If the CEO really doesn't get the practicalities of customer focus, you're on a road to nowhere and the company is probably doomed. Get out while you can.

■ ■ ■

You Are a Marketer

You have a passion for brands. You understand the market. You are your company's linchpin for customer focus, especially in this digital age.

If you choose, your spot in the organization *can* be exalted. Top management *will* respect and look to you as it makes key business decisions.

Success isn't primarily about your genes. With the help of many marketing leaders and experts, we've uncovered the 12 Powers of a marketing leader that will help you step up, take charge, and become influential.

The choice now is yours.

■ ■ ■

As you move forward, please let us know how things are going! We'd love to hear from you on www.marketingleader.org.

Good luck!
Thomas & Patrick

APPENDIX: ABOUT THE RESEARCH

The Marketer's DNA—Research Notes

The original research program on which this book is based, titled "The Marketer's DNA," comprised three complementary studies:

1. **Senior marketer study.** To explore how senior marketers' personalities, leadership behaviors, and functional skills affect their business impact and career success, we collected and analyzed detailed self-report data from 1,232 senior marketers from 71 countries. This study, designed and executed specifically for the book, generated the core results reported in each chapter.

2. **360-degree leadership study.** To complement the senior marketer study, we also analyzed existing 360-degree data on 626 marketing leaders and 6,803 other functional leaders (in finance, operations, sales, etc.), a total of 67,278 individual assessments of 7,429 marketing and nonmarketing leaders—an average of 9.1 per individual, including his/her self-assessment. This enabled us to analyze how marketing leaders (relative to other functional leaders) are perceived by their bosses, peers, and subordinates. It also provides a check on how senior marketers' self-perceptions compare with how others see them.

3. **Qualitative research interviews.** To supplement and help us interpret the two quantitative studies, and to illustrate the results, we also conducted 104 semi-structured depth interviews over the course of the project with senior marketers, CEOs, HR leaders, and leadership experts.

In the rest of this Appendix, we describe the background literature, the aims of the research program, and the details of each of the three studies.

Background: Company-Wide Market Orientation

As Drucker wrote more than sixty years ago, in the long term, companies succeed by profitably (a key word!) meeting their customers' needs better than the competition. They therefore need to keep improving, innovating, and adapting, while remaining relentlessly focused on customer needs. Drucker's argument has been repeatedly tested and validated, notably in an extensive research program by the Marketing Science Institute in the 1980s. More recently, a large global study of top management teams by Egon Zehnder and McKinsey (2011) found that, among all leadership behaviors, the top team's customer focus was the number one predictor of company growth.

Two widely cited conceptualizations of Drucker's marketing concept emerged from the MSI program. Kohli and Jaworski (1990) focused on the "organization-wide generation and dissemination of market intelligence, and the company's responsiveness to it." Narver and Slater (1990) focused on three key dimensions of a market-oriented organizational culture: "customer orientation, competitor orientation, and inter-functional coordination." Both approaches emphasize that market orientation applies to the whole organization. This suggests that the way the marketing team relates to other departments may be at least as important as its functional expertise and performance (e.g., how well it spends the marketing budget).

Later research has supported this view. For instance, Wong and Tong's (2012) study of the influence of market orientation on new product success found that inter-functional coordination, especially between marketing and R&D, had the most significant impact on the probability of success.

Marketers' Role and Influence

Although market orientation relates to the whole organization, marketers have a particular role in helping companies become more customer-focused and ensuring that innovation priorities are relevant to the market. This role comprises:

1. Understanding customers' often subtle, and continuously evolving, needs
2. Monitoring key competitors' activity and performance
3. Feeding this understanding into the company's innovation and delivery activities
4. Communicating the resulting offer to customers and prospects in a way that, ideally, engages their emotions as well as matching their rational and functional needs
5. Monitoring customers' experience of, and responses to, their interactions with the company and its products and services
6. Helping to ensure that the brand promise stays relevant and competitive and that the delivery reliably matches that promise

Given the importance of this role in creating and retaining profitable customers—the central task of business—you'd think marketers would have huge influence within the company and be respectfully listened to at the top table. But this is rarely what happens. Instead, in many companies, their influence is quite limited:

- A widely read 2004 article by consultants Booz Allen Hamilton asked, "Are CMOs irrelevant?"
- When asked about their greatest challenge, 53 percent of technology CMOs pointed to cross-functional issues. Too often, they had to "educate the entire organization, including senior management, with regard to the role and/or value of the marketing function relative to the achievement of their company's strategic vision" (Koleszar and Bernhardt, 2009).

■ A 2012 study of 200 top marketing leaders, by Forrester Research and executive search firm Heidrick & Struggles, concluded that, while senior marketers are slowly "moving from the outskirts to the core of the enterprise," much more needs to be done to "change the mindset of their executive peers regarding the role of marketing."

These are not new challenges. As long ago as 1948, marketing professor James W. Culliton wrote: "The difficulty arises not just because of the incomplete understanding of the general concept of marketing, but also and particularly because of the confusion about what specific items of expenditure a business should count as marketing cost."

Responding to these Challenges

The question for senior marketers is what to do about these long-term "organizational" challenges—while still addressing the increasingly complex and fast-changing "technical" challenges in marketing (digital and mobile; big data aggregation; analytics; privacy and security; fast-changing customer needs and distribution channels, etc.).

There has been limited relevant academic research: "leadership is rarely discussed in the marketing literature" (Scott, 2012). In 2008, Professors Pravin Nath (Drexel University) and Vijay Mahajan (University of Texas, Austin) found no simple relationship between company performance and the presence of a CMO in the top management team. However, a follow-up study by Germann, Ebbes, and Grewal (2015) found that companies with CMOs in the top team are significantly more profitable (15 percent higher Tobin's Q than those without, other things being equal). And the most recent study by Feng and colleagues (2015) found that a powerful marketing department has a clear positive impact on long-term stock returns and short-term return on assets (ROA) for US firms. We hope that other scholars will further explore this important issue.

As far as we know, however, there has been no previous academic research on the determinants of *marketers'* business impact and career success. That is why we decided to conduct our own research. The aims were to uncover these determinants so that our book could use the results to advise marketers on how to maximize their influence, their contribution to the company's business performance, and, ultimately, their personal career success.

1. Senior Marketer Study

Inevitably, some marketers are more successful than others at coping with the challenges discussed here. Our main study, using self-report data from 1,232 senior marketers, aimed to exploit this variation by exploring the behaviors and other factors associated with senior marketers' business impact and career success.

Research Questions

This study addressed three specific research questions:

1. Which leadership behaviors, personality traits, and functional marketing skills best account for senior marketers' business impact and career success?
2. Which external organizational factors also affect these outcomes?
3. How do senior marketing leaders perceive their own performance and situation with regards to leadership behaviors, personality traits, functional marketing skills, and organizational factors?

Marketing Leadership Model

Some previous researchers have highlighted the transformational nature of the marketing role. Scott (2012), for example, in a study of over 1,000 US executives, concluded that marketing leaders first and foremost need *charisma, intelligence, vision,* and *integrity*—traits closely associated with *transformational leadership.* Several other authors highlight the transformational character of the marketing role, especially the focus on fostering company growth (Spencer Stuart, 2010). The transformational view is also supported by Aaker (2008), who suggests in his book

Spanning Silos that "the central marketing group must engage the whole organization."

Kets de Vries's book *The Leadership Mystique: Leading Behavior in the Human Enterprise* (2006) argues that leaders must play both a "charismatic" role and an "architectural" role. They also need emotional stability, task-relevant knowledge, and a number of generic leadership skills such as self-management, cultural relativity, team management, and trust building.

Kets de Vries's approach is summarized in his Digital Leadership Model (DLM). We selected the DLM as the starting point for the development of our own measurement model development for several reasons. The DLM is a contemporary transformational leadership model. Its leadership dimensions closely match the demands on marketers. Kets de Vries has validated it using an associated 360-degree leadership assessment instrument (GELI—see "Research Questions," page 203). His team was also happy to give us access to their large 360-degree database, so we could conduct further analyses to validate and extend our core research.

To ensure good alignment between our model and marketers' real-world challenges, however, we carried out significant qualitative research to adjust and supplement DLM with, for example, functional skills like strategic pricing, brand positioning, or data mining. We conducted an initial program of forty-one semi-structured interviews with CMOs, CEOs, HR experts, and marketing experts. We asked them to assign importance weights to our (extended DLM) leadership dimensions and to suggest additional ones where necessary. We also collected stories about leaders' successes and failures that might be helpful in illustrating specific points in the book.

The interviews confirmed most dimensions of our initial marketing leadership model. However, the interviewees helped us add important functional skills (e.g., tactical pricing) and marketing leadership behaviors (e.g., return orientation). They also made numerous suggestions on how to phrase statements to make them clear and to ensure that they reflect marketers' working reality.

During the qualitative interviews, one question often came up: Are the best marketing leaders "born" or "made"? To help answer this, we added the Big Five Personality Inventory (Costa and McCrae, 1992) to our leadership model. This widely used personality model consists of five personality dimensions: openness to experience, conscientiousness, extraversion, agreeableness, and emotional stability. To keep it simple, we used an abbreviated eight-statement version of the Big Five (TIPI), developed and validated by Gosling, Rentfrow, and Swann (2003).

Based on the interviews, and with helpful input from INSEAD professors Roger Lehman and Eric Van De Loo, our final marketing leadership model comprised ninety-six statements covering each respondent's self-reported leadership behaviors, personality, functional skills, support, career success, and business success.

Twenty-seven of the statements were similar to those of Kets de Vries's 360-degree assessment (GELI—based on the DLM model). Sixty-one, based on our qualitative interviews, were about respondents' specific marketing skills, behaviors, attitudes, business impact, career success, and support/resources. The other eight were from the TIPI personality instrument. Examples include:

- (Behaviors) "I am very focused; I work mostly on my top priorities."
- (Personality—TIPI) "I see myself as extraverted, enthusiastic."
- (Skills) "Colleagues would say that I (or my team) master tactical pricing very well."
- (Support/Resources) "I currently have the people and funds needed in order to win in the market."
- (Success) "My career is developing well. I like where it's going."

With the help of the US-based CMO Council, *absatzwirtschaft*, a leading German marketing magazine, and personal contacts, we recruited 1,232 senior marketers from a wide range of mid-size and large companies in sixteen different B2B and B2C industries and seventy-one countries.

Participants were asked, in confidence, how well each of the ninety-six statements described them and their situation using a six-point Likert scale (1 = not at all, 6 = very well). They were promised absolute confidentiality, encouraging honest responses.

We used a proprietary web-based graphical interface developed for us by Axel Puhlmann at research company cognoscenti. This allowed fast, single-click responses, increasing the completion rate and significantly reducing errors. Each respondent also received an immediate summary report of his or her personal results, further encouraging participation. The final sample broke down as follows:

Seniority	Percentage
CEO/President/Owner	8.8
VP/Director/Head of Department	53.4
Senior Manager or equivalent	28.8
Manager or equivalent	9.0
Geography	
Europe	53.7
Asia	20.0
North America	16.2
Rest of World	10.1*
Marketing Focus	
Business (B2B)	60.2
Consumers (B2C)	39.8

For the analysis, we weighted the data geographically, using population data, to get as close as possible to a globally representative sample of senior marketers. Using these data, we then established which leadership behaviors, personality traits, and marketing skills account for senior marketers' self-reported business impact and career success.

Analytics expert Dr. Frank Buckler (www.causalanalytics.com) applied universal structure modeling to the data. Frank used a new neural network-based causal analytics algorithm (NEUSREL) to estimate the network of causal relations between the ninety-six variables, allowing for the possibility of unknown nonlinearities and interactions.

---

* Africa 1.9%, Latin America 2.8%, Middle East 3.0%, Australia/NZ/Oceania 2.3%.

The model achieved R^2s of 0.46 for business impact and 0.59 for career success.* Given that our model excludes many aspects of organizational and market context that drive business and personal success, these R^2s were highly satisfactory and, because of the large sample size, all the results reported through the book are statistically significant at the 0.05 confidence level or better.†

We used statistical techniques (a Principal Components Analysis with Promax rotation and Kaiser-normalizing) to reduce the results to the four-component solution which also informed the structure and narrative for the book (boss, colleagues, team, self).

2. 360-Degree Leadership Study

The overall aim of this second study was to evaluate how senior marketers are perceived by their bosses, peers, and subordinates across 100 measures, compared with the equivalent for leaders of six other functions (i.e., relative to how the latter are perceived by *their* bosses, peers, and subordinates using the same measures). The other functions were general management, finance, operations, sales, HR, and IT.

Research Questions

The study was mainly designed to address two research questions:

1. Are marketing leaders really less satisfied with their career progress than other functional leaders, as suggested by previous research?
2. How do their bosses view marketing leaders (relative to how bosses view their other direct reports) in terms of career success?

---

* The R^2 is a statistical measure of the proportion of the variation in a dependent variable accounted for by the model. The model included the variables that became the 12 Powers, eight organizational role variables, and 13 other variables reflecting firm and individual demographics. Neural network models do not apportion variance but, using Buckler and Hennig-Thurau's (2008) Overall Explained Absolute Deviation (OEAD) measure, the 12 Powers accounted for about 63 percent of the R^2 for business impact and 49 percent for career success. The organizational role variables accounted for around 21 percent of the variance in business impact and 35 percent for career success. The rest (about 16 percent for both outcomes) was accounted for by the demographic variables.

† That is, for the results reported, there is at most a 5 percent chance that the result could be due to sampling error rather than a real effect.

What, in their view, are the factors driving and inhibiting these? Do they see any specific factors that are holding marketers back?

INSEAD's Global Leadership Center graciously gave us access to their 360-degree assessment database (www.gelionline.com/geli). The Global Leadership Inventory (GELI) is a 360-degree feedback instrument developed by Manfred Kets de Vries, Pierre Vrignaud, and Elizabeth Florent-Treacy (2004). It measures degrees of competency with 100 statements using a seven-point Likert scale (from 1—"Does not describe me at all" to 7—"Describes me completely") across twelve dimensions of global leadership: designing and aligning, envisioning, emotional intelligence, empowering, energizing, global mindset, life balance, outside orientation, resistance to stress, rewarding and feedback, team building, and tenacity.

We identified and labeled the functional roles of GELI participants based on their job titles, so that we could compare marketers against other functional leaders. We were able to identify the functional roles of 7,429 target individuals (senior leaders/managers) from 178 countries, and 52 industries, leading to 67,278 usable 360-degree assessments. The distribution of our 360-degree data sample was as follows:

Role	
Bosses	8,756
Peers	19,579
Subordinates	22,477
Others*	9,037
Self	7,429
Total	67,278
Roles of Observed Individuals	
CEO/General Manager	2,708
Finance	1,118
Operations	1,054
Sales	790

* For example, other leaders with no reporting relationship, external mentors.

Marketing	626
HR	407
IT	200
Others	526*
Total	7,429

For each individual, we analyzed data from the individual him/herself and an average of eight colleagues: bosses, coworkers, direct reports, and others.

The results gave further hints as to why so many marketers are struggling in their careers—and how they can step up their efforts to become more influential and successful. We found that on average, the marketers enjoyed lower career satisfaction than *any* of the other senior executives. In line with this somewhat alarming finding, bosses and peers (and, to a lesser extent, subordinates) rated the marketers lower than most other leaders across more than half of the 100 leadership attributes.

It appears that marketers' standing in many organizations isn't as strong as it could be and their unfavorable career progression is widely visible.

3. Qualitative Research Interviews

Throughout the project, we continued interviewing senior marketers to add perspectives and personal experiences to our insights. Forty-one structured interviews, with CMOs, CEOs, and HR/leadership experts, helped us shape our core research. Each interview started with a twenty-minute introduction where the participants described their current role and shared personal examples of marketing leadership success and failure. All interviewees then rated the importance of each of the proposed dimensions of the marketing leadership model on a four-point scale (1 = less important; 2 = important; 3 = very important; 4 = truly differentiating). Participants could, in addition, make suggestions for missing

---

* Marketing & Sales: 110; Legal: 194; Procurement: 92; R&D: 110; Strategy: 20.

items and clearer wording for the existing items. The quantitative ratings, together with the suggested additions and wording changes, informed the final modification of Kets de Vries's leadership model used in the main study. The book also contains insights from sixty-three later interviews with CMOs, CEOs, and senior marketers.

These qualitative interviews helped us challenge our research findings, explain the phenomena we observed (e.g., why marketers love working inside the marketing silo), and add stories to help us communicate our findings.

■　■　■

To the best of our knowledge, we have conducted the largest study to date into leadership in marketing. The work helped us uncover the most critical leadership behaviors for marketers' business impact and career success.

Given marketing's importance for business success and the current high career-failure rate of marketers, much more needs to be understood and done to help marketers succeed. We hope our work encourages other researchers to challenge, expand, and add to our findings.

SOURCES

Aaker, D. *Spanning Silos: The New CMO Imperative* (Cambridge, MA: Harvard Business Press, 2008).

Abernathy, J., Kubick, T., and Masli, A. "The Economic Relevance of Chief Marketing Officers in Firms' Top Management Teams," *Journal of Business & Economics Research*, vol. 11, no. 12 [December 2013].

Alsever, A., Hempel, J., Taylor, A., and Roberts, D. "6 Great Teams That Take Care of Business" (*see* "Execs Who Play (and Stay) Together), *Fortune* [April 28, 2014]: 38–9.

Barta, T., Kleinert, M., and Neumann, T. "Is There a Payoff from Top-Team Diversity?" *McKinsey Quarterly*, April 2012.

Barwise, P. "Brands & CEOs," The Brands Lecture 2015. British Brands Group, November 2015, http://www.britishbrandsgroup.org.uk/upload/File/2015%20 Brands%20Lecture.pdf.

Barwise, P. and Meehan, S. *Simply Better: Winning and Keeping Customers by Delivering What Matters Most* (Cambridge, MA: Harvard Business Press, 2004).

Barwise, P. and Meehan, S. *Beyond the Familiar: Long-Term Growth Through Customer Focus and Innovation* (San Francisco: Jossey-Bass, 2011).

Barwise, P. and Meehan, S. "The One Thing You Must Get Right When Building a Brand," *Harvard Business Review* [December 2010].

Bass, B. M. and Avolio, B. J. *Increasing Organizational Effectiveness Through Transformational Leadership* (Sage Publications, Inc., 1994).

Baumann, R. "Starting a New Job," *Business Strategy Review* [1995].

BCG Perspectives. "PepsiCo's Salman Amin on Building Global Brands in the Digital Age," company publication [2012].

Biesdorf, F., Court, D., and Willmott, P. "Big Data: What Is Your Plan?" *McKinsey Quarterly* [2013].

Booz Allen Hamilton. "Are CMOs Irrelevant?" Booz Allen Hamilton company publication (2004).

Bowles, M. "Logos and Eros: The Vital Syzygy for Understanding Human Relations and Organizational Action," *Human Relations,* vol. 46, issue 11 [November 1993]: 1271–90.

Bryant, A. "Having a Touch of Grace Helps Ground You," *New York Times,* April 21, 2014, page 1.

Buckler, F. and Hennig-Thurau, T., "Identifying Hidden Structures in Marketing's Structural Models through Universal Structure Modeling," *Marketing–Journal of Research and Management,* vol. 4, no. 2 [2008]: 47–66.

Buckler, F. *Das Ende der Kennzahlen-Illusion* (Münster, Germany: Monsenstein und Vannerdat, 2014).

Bulik, B. S. "CMOs Struggle to Acclimate to Changing Landscape," *Advertising Age* [Oct. 11, 2011]. Retrieved from: www.adage.com.

Burke, R. J. and Copper, C. L. *Inspiring Leaders* (Abingdon, UK: Routledge, 2006).

Burns, J. M. *Leadership* (New York: Harper & Row, 1978).

Capgemini "The Deciding Factor: Big Data & Decision Making," company publication (2012).

Collins, J. C. and Porras, J. I. "Building Your Company's Vision," *Harvard Business Review* [September/October 1996].

Costa, P. T. and McCrae, R. R. *Revised NEO Personality Inventory (NEO-PI-R) and NEO Five-Factor Inventory (NEO-FFI)* (Psychological Assessment Resources, 1992).

Covey, S. *The 7 Habits of Highly Effective People* (New York: Simon & Schuster, 1989).

Cox, R. "Three-in-One Marketing," *Harvard Business Review* [November/December 1956]: 61–8.

Culliton, J. "The Management Challenge of Marketing Costs," *Harvard Business Review* [January 1948]: 74.

Cumeau, J-B., Fletcher, B., and French, T. "Engaging Boards in the Future of Marketing," *McKinsey Quarterly* [February 2013].

Dahr, R. "Salman Amin, COO, SC Johnson & Son," Yale School of Management (2013). Retrieved from: som.yale.edu/salman-amin-coo-sc-johnson-son.

Dewhurst, M., Gutheridge, M., and Mohr, E. "Motivating People—Getting Beyond Money," *McKinsey Quarterly* [Nov. 2009].

Economist Intelligence Unit. "Outside Looking In: The CMO Struggles to Get in Sync with the C-suite," company report (2012).

Egon Zehnder International and McKinsey & Company. "Return on Leadership—Competencies that Generate Growth," company publication (2011).

Eisenhardt, K. M., Kahwajy. J. L., and Bourgeois III, L. J. "How Management Teams Can Have a Good Fight," *Harvard Business Review* [July/August 1997].

Elliott, K., Ricklefs, R., Gaston, A., Hatch, S., Speakmane, J., and Davorena, G. "High Flight Costs, But Low Dive Costs, in Auks Support the Biomechanical Hypothesis for Flightlessness in Penguins," proceedings of the National Academy of Sciences of the United States of America (2013).

Feng, H., Morgan, A. M., Rego, L. L. "Marketing Department Power and Firm Performance," *Journal of Marketing,* vol. 79, no. 5 [September 2015]: 1–20.

Folisi, S. *Eros Over Logos: A Revolt of the Instinctual Mind Amidst the Madness of Modernity* (Xander Stone Ink, 2012).

Frankfurter Allgeneine Sonntagszeitung (2012). Unsere Kunden sind Stammesbrüder. Modemanager John Flynn, Chef von Fred Perry, über Treue zur britischen Kultmarke, Musiker in Poloshorts und unerwünschte Fans. August 19, Nr. 33.

Freeling, A. *Agile Marketing: How to Innovate Faster, Cheaper and with Lower Risk* (Fairford, UK: Goldingtons Press, 2011).

Gawande, A. *The Checklist Manifesto: How to Get Things Right* (New York: Henry Holt, 2011).

Germann, F., Ebbes, P., and Grewal, R. "The Chief Marketing Officer Matters!", *Journal of Marketing,* vol. 79, no. 1 [May 2015]: 1–22.

Gilyard, B. "Interview with Mark Addicks, Senior Vice President and Chief Marketing Officer, General Mills, *Twin Cities Business* [Nov. 22, 2013]. Retrieved from tcbmag.com/Leadership/Leaders/The-Interview-Issue.

Gosling, S. D., Rentfrow, P. J., and Swann, W. B., Jr. "A Very Brief Measure of the Big Five Personality Domains," *Journal of Research in Personality,* vol. 37 [2003]: 504–28.

Granatstein, L. "How 6 Powerful Women in Media and Marketing Redefined the Rules of Leadership," *Adweek* [Sept. 27, 2015]. Retrieved from: www.adweek

.com/news/advertising-branding/how-6-powerful-women-media-and-marketing-redefined-rules-leadership-167182.

Groysberg, B., Kelly, L., and MacDonald, B. "The New Path to the C-Suite," *Harvard Business Review* [March 2011].

Hanna, R. "Personal Meaning: Its Loss and Rediscovery," *Human Systems Development*, R. Tannenbaum, et al., eds. (San Francisco: Jossey-Bass, 1985).

Harter, G., Landry, E., and Tipping, A. "The New Complete Marketer," *Strategy+Business,* issue 48 [Autumn 2007].

Hastie, T., Tibshirani, R., and Friedman, J. *The Elements of Statistical Learning* (Springer, 2009).

Hill, L. *Becoming a Manager: Mastery of a New Identity* (Harvard Business Press, 1992).

Homburg, C., Vomberg, A., Enke, M., and Grimm, P. "The Loss of the Marketing Department's Influence: Is It Really Happening? And Why Worry?" *Journal of the Academy of Marketing Science,* vol. 43 [November 2014]: 1–13.

Ibarra, H. *Working Identity: Unconventional Strategies for Reinventing Your Career* (Harvard Business Press, 2003).

IBM. "From Stretched to Strengthened: Insights from the Global Chief Marketing Officer Study," company publication (2012).

IRI. "New Pacesetters 100: The Fuel to Accelerate Growth," company publication (April 2013).

Iyer, B. "CMO Colours Lenovo Brand," Campaign Asia [Sept. 29, 2015]. Retrieved from www.campaignasia.com/Article/402328,CMO+colours+Lenovo+brand.aspx.

Jung, C. G. *Aspects of the Feminine* (Abingdon, UK: Routledge, 1982).

Kakabadse, N. K., Kakabadse A., and Lee-Davis, L. "Visioning the Pathway: A Process Model," *European Management Journal,* vol. 23, no. 2 [2005]: 237–46.

Katzenbach, J. "The Steve Jobs Way," *Strategy + Business,* issue 67 [Summer 2012].

Kets de Vries, M., Virgnaud, P., and Forent-Treacy, E. "The Global Life Inventory: Development and Psychometric Properties of a 360-Degree Feedback Instrument," *The International Journal of Human Resource Management* [May 2004]: 475–92.

Kets de Vries, M. *The Leadership Mystique: Leading Behavior in the Human Enterprise* (Upper Saddle River, NJ: Prentice Hall, 2006).

Kirklund, Rik. "Leading in the 21st Century: An Interview with Ford's Alan Mulally," McKinsey.com [Nov. 2013]. Retrieved from www.mckinsey.com/insights/strategy/leading_in_the_21st_century_an_interview_with_fords_alan_mulally.

Kohli, A. K. and Jaworski, B. J. "Market Orientation: The Construct, Research Propositions and Managerial Implications," *Journal of Marketing,* vol. 54, no. 2 [April 1990]: 1–18.

Kolesnikov-Jessop, Sonia. "Make People Believe in Themselves, Questions for Ian Harebottle, the chief executive of the Gemfields mining company." *New York Times,* April 28, 2014.

Kolesnikov-Jessop, S. "At Career's End, Calvin Klein's Chief Executive Prepares for Transition," *New York Times,* May 12, 2014.

Koleszar, W. L. and Bernhardt, K. L. "The Role & Leadership Challenges of the Chief Marketing Officer: A Study of High-Tech CMOs," private publication (2009).

Korn/Ferry Institute. "The Transformative CMO," March 2012.

Korn/Ferry Institute. "Marketing Pulse Survey," 2013.

Kotler, P., Rackham, N., and Krishnaswamy, S. "Ending the War Between Sales & Marketing," *Harvard Business Review* [May 2009].

Kotter, J. P. "Leading Change: Why Transformation Efforts Fail," *Harvard Business Review* [January 2007].

Kotter J. "How to Create a Powerful Vision for Change," Forbes.com, retrieved from www.forbes.com/sites/johnkotter/2011/06/07/how-to-create-a-powerful-vision-for-change.

Lafley, A. G. "P&G's Innovation Culture," *Strategy+Business,* issue 52 [Autumn 2008, reprint 08304].

Langley, M. "Inside Mulally's 'War Room': A Radical Overhaul of Ford," *Wall Street Journal* [Dec. 22, 2006]. Retrieved from: www.wsj.com/articles/SB116675864434457508.

Linton, M. "Why Do Chief Marketing Officers Have a Short Shelf Life?" *Forbes CMO Calculus* [May 2009].

Macleod, C. "TfL's Marketing Director: Why Marketers Must Create a Customer Focus to Become CEOs," *Marketing Week* [Aug. 24, 2015]. Retrieved from: www.marketingweek.com/2015/08/24/tfls-marketing-director-why-marketers-must-create-a-customer-focus-to-become-ceos.

Maister, D. H. *Managing the Professional Service Firm* (New York: Free Press, 1997).

Manzoni, J.-F. and Barsoux, J.-L. *The Set-Up-to-Fail Syndrome* (Cambridge, MA: Harvard Business Publishing, 2007).

McGovern, G. and Quelch, J. "The Fall and Rise of the CMO," *Strategy+Business*, issue 37 [winter 2004].

Meier, M. M. and Wichert, C. *Die Erfolgsgeheimnisse des Marketingmanagers* (Wiesbaden, Germany: Springer Gabler, 2010).

Meyer, A. M. "Does Matrix Management Replace the Organizational Hierarchy in Cross-Functional Brand Teams? A Case Study from the Bio-Pharmaceutical Industry," *International Journal of Economics and Management Sciences*, vol. 2, no. 12 [2013]: 52–6.

Narver, J. C. and Slater, S. F. "The Effect of a Market Orientation on Business Profitability," *Journal of Marketing*, vol. 54, no. 2 [1990]: 20–34.

Nath, N., Mahajan. V. "Chief Marketing Officers: A Study of Their Presence in Firms' Top Management Teams," *Journal of Marketing*, vol. 72, no. 1 [January 2008]: 65–81.

Nath, P. and Mahajan, V. "Marketing in the C-Suite: A Study of Chief Marketing Officer Power in Firms' Top Management Teams," *Journal of Marketing*, vol. 75, no. 1 [January 2011]: 60–77.

Osborne, A. "Bart Becht: The Man Who Cleaned Up at Reckitt Benckiser," *The Daily Telegraph*, Dec. 8, 2011.

Popelka, L. "Why Geeks Are the Best Marketers," *Bloomberg Businessweek* [November, 8, 2011].

Roderick, L. "Why Marketers Are Failing to Get a Place in the Boardroom," *Marketing Week* [Sept. 30, 2015]. Retrieved from: www.marketingweek.com/2015/09/30/why-marketers-are-failing-to-get-a-place-in-the-boardroom.

Scott, C. J. "Leadership Perceptions in the Marketing Organization and Technological Uncertainty," *Journal of Marketing Development and Competitiveness*, vol. 6, no. 1 [2012]: 11–19.

Spencer Stuart. "What Do You Want from Me? How High Performing CMOs Exceed Expectations," company publication (2010).

Spencer Stuart. "Big Data and the CMO: What's Changing for Marketing Leadership?" company publication (2010).

Spencer Stuart. "The Rising CMO," company publication (2010).

Spencer Stuart. "The Role of Today's Chief Marketing Officer," company publication (2010).

Spencer Stuart. "Staying on the Cutting Edge: Innovation's Role in the Future of Marketing—CMO Summit Survey Results," company publication (2012).

Spencer Stuart. "Myths and Opportunities. How Marketers Can Position Themselves for a Board Role," company publication (2013).

Spencer Stuart. "Chief Marketing Officer Tenure Now at 45 Months," company press release (May 1, 2013).

Stein, S. J. and Book, H. E. *The EQ Edge: Emotional Intelligence and Your Success* (San Francisco: Jossey-Bass, 2011).

Stodgill, R. M. *Handbook of Leadership: A Survey of Theory and Research* (New York: Free Press, 1974).

Süddeustche Zeitung Magazin. "Hippie Eis," Interview with Ben Cohen and Jerry Greenfield [2013].

The Economist (Asia Edition). "Equal Opportunities in South Korea: Gladder to Be Gay. A Multinational's Job Advert Stirs Controversy," Economist.com [Oct. 22, 2011].

The Economist. The Adidas Method: A German Firm's Unusual Approach to Designing Its Products," Economist.com [Aug. 24, 2013].

The Marketing Academy "Creating a Recipe for a Strong, Successful Team: Careers Guide," academy publication (2013).

The Marketing Society. "Our Manifesto for Marketing Leadership: How to Become a Bolder Marketing Leader and Why It Matters," society publication (2015).

Thomke, S. and Reinertsen, D. "Six Myths of Product Development," *Harvard Business Review*, vol. 90, no. 5 [May 2012]: 84–94.

Thomke, S. and Von Hippel, E. "Customers as Innovators," *Harvard Business Review* [April 2002]: 74–81.

Weber, M. *Wirtschaft und Gesellschaft: Grundriss der verstehenden Soziologie* (Tübingen, Germany: Mohr Siebeck, 1922 and 2002).

West, L., and Milan, M. *The Reflecting Glass. Professional Coaching for Leadership Development* (New York: Palgrave Macmillan, 2001).

Wong, S. K. and Tong, C. "The Influence of Market Orientation on New Product Success," *European Journal of Innovation Management*, vol. 15 [2012], issue 1: 99–121.

ACKNOWLEDGMENTS

Our biggest thanks go to Thomas, Catherine, and the rest of our families, who have endured our frequent physical and mental absences as we were concentrating on the book. Many thanks also to Donya Dickerson, our inspiring editor, and her McGraw-Hill colleagues Courtney Fischer, Elena Christie, and Daina Penikas, for their help in making this book happen, and to Tom Miller, our agent who always believed in our project.

The insights and recommendations in this book are based on the Marketer's DNA research program described in the Appendix. We have many people to thank for enabling us to give this book a solid research foundation.

First and foremost, thank you to the 1,232 CMOs and other senior marketers from around the globe who gave us, for the core of the Marketer's DNA research, confidential—and, on some dimensions, highly personal—insights into their personalities, roles, and careers.

We would like to acknowledge the generous support of the leadership faculty at INSEAD (Fontainebleau, France, and Singapore). Professors Manfred Kets de Vries, Roger Lehman, Eric van de Loo, and Elizabeth Florent-Treacy encouraged us and provided critical input throughout the project. Manfred and Elizabeth also kindly gave us access to their large global 360-degree database, enabling us to check, supplement, and contextualize with the help of 67,287 leadership assessments the results of our core senior marketer study.

Many CMOs, CEOs, and leadership experts helped us with their advice, experiences, and suggestions. Thank you, in particular, to Mark Addicks, Salman Amin, Wolfgang Baier, Anna Bateson, Nand Kishore Badami, Wendy Becker, Roberto Berardi, Harald Bellm, John Bernard, Maxim Bonpain, Tim Brooks, Michael Chivers, Abigail Comber, Sonia

Devito, Sholto Douglas-Home, Dee Dutta, Prasert Eamrungroj, Jim Farley, Anthony Freeling, Marshall Goldsmith, Harriett Green, David James, Benjamin Karsch, Simon Kang, Indy Kaur, Chris Macleod, Bernhard Mattes, Michael M. Meier, Christoph Michalski, Jean-Francois Manzoni, Tina Müller, Winnie Palmer, Bob Scaglione, Alexander Schlaubitz, Ed Smith, Denis Schrey, Kiyoshi Saito, Luc Viardot, Steve Walker, and Bob Wooton, and the many other senior leaders we spoke to within the Marketer's DNA research program. A personal thanks to Hajo Riesenbeck, Jesko Perrey, and Trond Riiber Knudsen, Thomas's former colleagues at McKinsey, whose work first inspired him—and many CMOs—to take a top management view of marketing.

We are also grateful to Christoph Berdi and Christian Thunig, of the leading German marketing magazine *absatzwirtschaft*, to Donovan Neale-May, Matt Martini, and Liz Miller of the CMO Council, and to our many personal contacts for their help in recruiting the large global sample for our senior marketer study.

A big thank-you also to Thomas's peers in the INSEAD CCC Program for their critical input into the research design: Jamil Awaida, Nadeem Abdul Azeez, Yves Braibant, Florence Bernet, Kushal Bhomick, Carl Bou Malham, Ziv Carmon, Christoph Grimont, Alexandra Hope, Andrew Jones, Naveen Khajanchi, Sarang Kir, Natalie Rob, and Camilla Sudgen.

We couldn't have done our study without two outstanding experts. Dr. Frank Buckler, of analytics company Success Drivers, developed a tailored neural network model for us and used it to analyze the data, uncovering the critical factors that became the 12 Powers of a Marketing Leader described in the book. Axel Puhlmann, of research firm cognoscenti, developed the respondent interface for the senior marketer study, significantly contributing to the high quality of the responses.

The research is only part of the story. Writing a book is another. Mark Levy and Kelly McKain did a great job helping us turn Thomas's "German English" and Paddy's British precision into a readable book. Bianca and Günter Lampert, together with their team at alpine hotel Kaiserhof created the perfect writing retreat for Thomas.

Thanks also to all those who kindly read and commented on the earlier drafts: April Adams-Redmond, Tim Ambler, Alex Barwise, Andy Bird, Hugh Burkitt, Bram Clicke, Peter Corijn, Matt Day, Markus Daub, Aniko Delaney, Sonia Devito, Alexandra Dick, Dee Dutta, Paul Feldwick, David French, Indy Kaur, Georg Klein, Claudia Kunath, Thomas Lang, Keith McCambridge, Seán Meehan, Will Moore, Christine Moreman, Julia Porter, Ruth Saunders, Ginny Too, Bob Wootton, and John Zealley. We hope you'll see from the final version how your comments made a real difference.

Finally, there's no point writing a book if no one knows about it. Barbara Henricks, Jessica Krakoski, Rusty Shelton, and Paige Dillon were instrumental in creating the outreach we needed. Without their help, you might not be reading this.

INDEX

Note: page numbers followed by "f" and "t" indicate figures and tables, respectively.

Accountability. *See* Let the Outcomes
    Speak
Addicks, Mark, 53
Adidas, 58, 59, 61, 157
Aim Higher (vision) (Power #12),
    183–189
    case study (LG), 183–184
    central question, 183
    contribution to impact and success, 8t,
        185, 185f
    critical questions to answer, 189
    importance of, 185–187
    inspirational power of vision, 184–185
    Marketing Leadership Manifestos,
        187–189
    statistics, 186
Akzo Nobel, 134–136
Alignment of teams, 108–112
Amin, Salman, 108, 157
Apple, 26–27, 57–58, 123, 172
Authenticity, effective, 178–182
Authority, 121, 136

Badami, Nand Kishore, 22
Baier, Wolfgang, 90, 153
Barsoux, Jean-Louis, 129
Bateson, Anna, 44
Becht, Bart, 156
Ben & Jerry's, 27
Bennis, Warren, 63

Berardi, Roberto, 162
Berkshire Hathaway, 52
Bernard, John, 54
"Big bang" customer issues, 26–27
Big data, 158–161. *See also* Data
Big Three leadership behaviors, 192
Bisphenol A, 135
BMO Harris Bank, 52
Bonus structure, 143
Boss, mobilizing. *See* Deliver Returns,
    No Matter What; Tackle Only
    Big Issues; Work Only with the
    Best
British Airways, 47
BT Sport, 79–80
Buckler, Frank, 203
Budgets, 53, 54
Buffett, Warren, 52
Bulldozer war cabinet, 81–82
Business impact
    12 powers, contribution of, 6–8, 7–8t
    big issues, 7t, 19–21, 20f
    going first, 7t, 85, 86f
    inspirational self-awareness, 8t, 171,
        171f
    knowledge, 8t, 151f, 155
    performance and accountability, 8t,
        131, 132f
    returns, 7t, 43, 43f
    storytelling, 66, 67f
    team skills mix, 7t, 98, 98f
    trust, 8t, 116, 116f
    vision, 8t, 185, 185f

walking the halls, 7t, 75, 75f
working with the best, 7t, 59, 59t
Business Planning Review (BPR), 134

Camelot, 44, 89
Career planning and career maps,
    142–143
Career success of senior marketers
    12 powers, contribution of, 6–8, 7–8t
    big issues, 7t, 19–21, 20f
    going first, 7t, 85, 86f
    inspirational self-awareness, 8t, 171,
        171f
    knowledge, 8t, 151f, 155
    performance and accountability, 8t,
        131, 132f
    returns, 7t, 43, 43f
    storytelling, 66, 67f
    team skills mix, 7t, 98, 98f
    trust, 8t, 116, 116f
    vision, 8t, 185, 185f
    walking the halls, 7t, 75, 75f
    working with the best, 7t, 59, 59t
Celebrating success, 138
CFOs (Chief Financial Officers),
    partnering with, 46–48
Charisma, 170
"Chief mood officer," 129–130
Chivers, Michael, 163
CMOs (Chief Marketing Officers) and
    senior marketers
    how they speak about their role, 19–20
    mastering the powers (Truth #2), 6–8,
        7–8t
    personality vs. leadership skills, 8–10
    what they do, and profit drivers, 49,
        49t
Coaching and 70/30/0 rule, 126
Cohen, Ben, 27
Colgate, 25
Colleagues, mobilizing. See Hit the Head
    and the Heart; Walk the Halls; You
    Go First

Communication
    customer knowledge and, 155–156
    hearing everyone's voice, 125
    jargon, 89–90
    language of customers, 24, 70–71,
        89–90
    LDC ("Listen, Decide,
        Communicate"), 79–80
    new partners, talking to, 61–62
    revenue- or profitability-oriented, 90
Company needs, 21, 27–29. See also
    V-Zone
Competitive intelligence reporting,
    161–162
Conferences, 61, 162
Confidence-building, 123–128
Conflict management, 117–118, 128–130
Cook, Tim, 123
Coomber, Abigail, 47
Cornish, Sophie, 162–163
Cover Them in Trust (Power #8),
    115–130
    case study (IBM), 127
    case study (The Post Office, Britain),
        118–119
    central question, 115
    coaching and 70/30/0 rule, 126
    confidence-building, 123–128
    conflict management, 117–118,
        128–130
    contribution to impact and success, 8t,
        116, 116f
    critical questions to answer, 130
    delegation and, 115, 117, 119
    ego, controlling, 118, 123
    "forgiveness, not permission" rule,
        124–125
    "good fights," 126–128
    importance of, 115–116, 119, 120
    intimacy and, 120, 122–123
    professionalism and, 121–122
    statistics, 117
    trust equation, 119–120

Cross-functional work, 80
Culliton, James W., 198
Culture of performance, 136–138
Customer knowledge
    business ideas from talking to
        customers, 155–156
    case study ("David," steel
        manufacturing company),
        154–155
    contribution to impact and success,
        151f
    directly asking customers for help,
        156–157
    need for, 153
    from other departments, 153–155
    time spent with customers, 155
    turning data into insights, 157–161
Customers
    acquisition vs. retention of, 5
    "big bang" issues, 26–27
    customer surplus, 51
    digital strategy and, 36–37
    language of, 24, 70–71, 89–90
    marketing focus on, 5
    "simply better" customer issues and
        latent needs, 24–26

Data
    big issues and, 30–32
    customer insights from, 157–161
    on digital instruments, 38
    opinions vs., 127
    performance assessment and, 140–141
    success-based rewards and, 143
Data analysts, 160–161
Day, Matt, 164
Deadlines, 136, 137
"Decide," in LDC, 79
Delegation, 115, 117, 119
Deliver Returns, No Matter What
    (Power #2), 41–55
    case study ("Daniel," consumer
        electronics), 48–50

case study (Ford), 41–42
central question, 41
contribution to impact and success, 7t,
    43, 43f
critical questions to answer, 55
customer surplus and, 51
importance of, 43–44
influencing the most powerful
    marketing instruments, 48–51
investor, acting like, 52–54
partnering with finance and measuring
    return, 46–48
simple marketing models and getting
    into the revenue camp, 44–46, 45f
Del Real, Remberto, 52
Deming, Ed, 30
Digital Leadership Model (DLM), 200
Digital skills, 96–97, 99, 100f
Digital strategy, 35–39
Disagreement, constructive, 126–127
Distinctiveness, recruiting for, 102–105
Diversity on teams, 105
Douglas-Home, Sholto, 45, 109–110
Do Us a Flavour program (PepsiCo), 157
Drucker, Peter, 12, 196
Dulux, 164
Duncan, Andy, 44, 89
Dutta, Dee, 17–19, 23–24, 88

Ego, controlling, 118, 123
80/20 approach, 48
Eisenhardt, Kathleen, M., 126–127, 134
Elephant in the room, 80–81
Energy, testing, 29
Eros–Logos personality continuum,
    174–177
Evaluation. *See* Let the Outcomes Speak

Falling in Love with Your World
    (knowledge) (Power #10), 149–167
    case study ("David," steel
        manufacturing company),
        154–155

Falling in Love with Your World (*Cont.*)
    case study (PepsiCo), 157
    central question, 149
    contribution to impact and success, 8t, 151f, 152
    critical questions to answer, 166–167
    customer knowledge, 153–161
    as inspiration source, 149–153
    market understanding, 161–163
    product knowledge, 163–165
    statistics on marketer knowledgeability, 152–153
Farley, Jim, 41–42, 44, 66, 120
Firing, 143–144
Flynn, John, 25
Ford Motor Company, 23, 41–42, 67, 120, 134
"Forgiveness, not permission" rule, 124–125
Fred Perry, 25
Front line, getting to, 89
Future growth, highlighting sources of, 24

General Mills, 53
Get the Mix Right (team skills mix) (Power #7), 95–113
    alignment, 108–112
    case study (Hays and Millennium Experience, London), 109–110
    case study (PepsiCo), 108
    case study (Transport for London), 100–102
    central question, 95
    contribution to impact and success, 7t, 98, 98f
    critical questions to answer, 113
    distinctiveness, recruiting for, 102–105
    diversity, 105
    external focus, 112
    functional skills beyond marketing, 108
    importance of, 95–98
    make or buy?, 105–106

    marketing leadership skills, 106, 107
    networks and networking skills, 105
    prioritization workshops, 112
    skills-and-traits sheet, 104, 104t
    skills gaps, 99–100, 100f
    statistics, 98–99
    structured skills training, 107–108
    team mission, 111
Gilt, 122
Global Leadership Inventory (GELI), 204
GMOOT (Get Me One of Those), 82
Goal setting, 185
Godin, Seth, 85
Goldsmith, Marshall, 12
"Good enough" relationships, 129
Greenfield, Jerry, 27
Growth levers, 50

Harebottle, Ian, 124
Hays, 45, 109–110
Henkel, 87
Hershey, 52
Hit the Head and the Heart (storytelling) (Power #4), 65–71
    case study ("Jaime," door handle business), 67–69
    central question, 65
    contribution to impact and success, 7t, 66, 67f
    critical questions to answer, 71
    customer language, using, 70–71
    heart, head, and how-to elements of story, 69–70
    vision and, 66
V-Zone and, 65–66
Horst, Peter, 52
Hudson, Dawn, 124
Humor, use of, 128

IBM, 27, 127
Iceberg Model, 172–173, 173f
Incremental improvements, 25–26

Industry conferences, 61, 162
Information maps, 159
Innovations, 25, 26–27, 38, 128
Insights analysis, 158–161
Inspiration. *See also* Know How You
    Inspire
  inspiring through your own inspiration,
    150
  knowledge and, 149–153
  vision and, 184–185
Institute of Practitioners in Advertising
    (IPA), 102
Interdepartmental evaluations, 141–142
Intimacy, 120, 122–123
Investor, acting like, 52–54
Issues, big. *See* Tackle Only Big Issues
Ive, Jonathan, 26, 172

James, David, 79–80
Jargon, 89–90
Job descriptions, 138
Jobs, Steve, 26, 27, 57–58

Kang, Simon, 183–184, 185
Kets de Vries, Manfred, 200, 201, 204,
    206
Know How You Inspire (inspirational
    self-awareness) (Power #11),
    169–182
  case study ("Craig," Asian airline),
    180–181
  central question, 169
  confirming what makes you tick (step
    #1), 172–177
  contribution to impact and success, 8t,
    171, 171f
  critical questions to answer, 182
  effective authenticity, developing (step
    #3), 178–182
  Eros–Logos personality continuum,
    174–177
  finding out how you inspire others
    (step #2), 178

"know thyself," 169–172
  statistics, 171–172, 175–176
Knowledge. *See* Falling in Love with Your
    World

Lafley, Alan G., 156
Lao Tzu, 93
Latent needs, 24–26
Launching, 191–193
LDC ("Listen, Decide, Communicate"),
    78–80
Leadership in marketing, 1–14. *See also*
    specific powers
  defined, 1–3
  making it happen, 12
  mastering the powers (Truth #2), 6–8,
    7–8t
  personality vs. leadership skills, 8–10
  team leadership, transition to, 97
  V-Zone (Truth #1) and, 4–5
Lemkau, Kristin, 116, 139
Lenovo, 134
Let the Outcomes Speak (performance
    and accountability) (Power #9),
    131–145
  annual reviews, 140
  behavior and accountability, 139–140
  biting the bullet on firing, 143–144
  career planning and career maps,
    142–143
  case study ("Jessica," nonprofit
    organization), 143–144
  case study (Akzo Nobel), 134–136
  case study (Ford), 134
  central question, 131
  contribution to impact and success, 8t,
    131, 132f
  critical questions to answer, 145
  culture of performance, building,
    134–136
  evaluators from other departments,
    141–142
  power of facts, 134–136

Let the Outcomes Speak (*Cont.*)
  statistics, 131–134, 133f
  success-based rewards, 143
  targets and assessment, 140–141
LG, 54, 183–184
Listening, 78, 127
Logos and Eros, 174–177

Mackey, John, 103
Macleod, Christopher, 24, 100–102
"Make or buy?," 27–28, 105–106
Manifestos, 187–189
Manzoni, Jean-François, 129
The Marketer's DNA study, 195–206
  background literature, 196–197
  marketers' role and influence,
    197–198
  qualitative research interviews, 195,
    205–206
  responding to organization and
    technical challenges, 198–199
  senior marketer study, 195, 199–203
  360-degree leadership study, 195,
    203–205
Marketing funnel model, 45, 45f
Marketing Leadership Manifestos,
  187–189
Marketing models, simple, 44–46, 45f
Market knowledge, 161–163
Markey, Peter, 118–119
Mattes, Bernhard, 23
McDonald, Jill, 39
McKinsey, 11, 58, 96–97, 105, 196
Meaningful conversations, 80–81
Meeting minutes, 137
Meier, Michael M., 165
Millennium Experience, London,
  109–110
Mission statements, team, 111
Modha, Dharmendra, 127
Movement building. *See* You Go First
Mulally, Alan, 134
Müller, Tina, 87

Net Promoter Score (NPS), 32
Networks and networking, 105, 165
News Corp Australia, 73–74, 79
Notonthehighstreet.com, 162–163

Olympics (Summer 2012), 101–102
One2One, 18–19, 23–24, 88
Open-ended questions, 128
Outcomes. *See* Let the Outcomes Speak

Partners, new, 61–62
Peluso, Michelle, 122
PepsiCo, 108, 124, 157
Personality
  distinctive traits, 103, 104t
  Eros–Logos continuum, 174–177
  inspirational traits, 170, 173
  marketing leadership and, 8–10
  tests and inventories, 122, 173, 201
Pilot projects, 88–89
P&Ls, 165, 181
The Post Office (Britain), 118–119
Power gap, 9
Power structure, balanced, 127
Praise, sharing, 82–83
Price tag on big issues, 22–24, 23f,
    30–32
Pricing, 23, 99, 100f
Prioritization workshops, 112
Procter & Gamble (P&G), 27, 156
Product development and operations
    teams, 164
Product knowledge, 163–165
Professionalism, fostering, 121–122
Promises, keeping, 121

Rand, Paul, 58
Realism, 29
Reckitt Benckiser, 156
Recruiting for distinctiveness, 102–105
RED, 58, 59, 61
Reporting, simple, 32
Revenue camp, getting into, 44–46

Reviews, annual, 140. *See also* Let the Outcomes Speak
Revlon, 42
Rewards, success-based, 143
Reynolds, Nick, 134
Ritson, Mark, 19–20
Role model, acting as, 121–122
Rotation of team members, 108, 165
Rules, following, 121

Saito, Kiyoshi, 89
Sakaguchi, Rikko, 77
Sander, Jil, 60
Self, mobilizing. *See* Aim Higher; Falling in Love with Your World; Know How You Inspire
Self-assessment quiz, 13–14
Self-awareness. *See* Know How You Inspire
"Set up to fail" syndrome, 129
70/30/0 rule in meetings, 126
Shackell, Sherilyn, 6
"Simply better" customer needs, 24
Skills gap, 9, 99–100, 100f
Skinner, B. F., 139
Smith, Ed, 73–74, 79
Softbank, 89
Sony Ericsson, 77
Steinem, Gloria, 147
Storytelling, 66–71, 76–78
Success, celebrating, 138

Tackle Only Big Issues (Power #1), 17–39
    asking to lead the resolution team, 33–35
    "big bang" customer issues, 26–27
    case study (broadband company), 33–34
    case study (consumer goods firm), 34–35
    case study (Dee Dutta and One2One), 17–19, 23–24
    case study (financial institution), 21–22
    central question, 17
    contribution to impact and success, 7t, 19–21, 20f
    critical questions to answer, 39
    customer issues and latent needs, finding, 24–26
    data and metrics for, 30–32
    definition of "big issues," 17
    digital strategy as big issue, 35–39
    identifying, 22
    key company needs as seen by CEOs, 27–29
    price tag on, 22–24, 23f, 30–32
    targets and, 140
Tactics, 35, 37–38, 96–97
Talent. *See* Work Only with the Best
Tangerine, 172
Tangible results, 85, 140–141
Targets, 136, 140–141
Team, mobilizing. *See* Get the Mix Right; Inspiration; Let the Outcomes Speak; Trust
Team mission, 111
"Throw the biggest stone," 50, 54
Time to success, 29
T-Mobile, 18
Training, 107–108
Transport for London (TfL), 24, 100–102
Trust gap, 9
Tucker, Holly, 162–163
12 Powers, 6–8, 7–8t, 13–14. *See also specific powers*

Viardot, Luc, 134–136
Vision. *See* Aim Higher
V-Zone (Value Creation Zone)
    big issues inside (*See* Tackle Only Big Issues)
    common goals and, 127
    confidence and, 124
    defined, 4–5, 4f

V-Zone (Value Creation Zone) (*Cont.*)
  digital and, 36
  enlarging, 8t, 18, 36, 65–66, 75, 90
  language and, 90
  recruiting and V-Zone challenge, 103
  repeating the story and, 77
  returns and, 50
  team mission and, 111

Walker, Steve, 77
Walk the Halls (Power #5), 73–83
  bulldozer war cabinet, 81–82
  case study (BT Sport), 79–80
  case study (News Corp Australia),
    73–74
  case study (Sony Ericsson), 77
  central question, 73
  contribution to impact and success, 7t,
    75, 75f
  critical questions to answer, 83
  cross-functional work, 80
  elephant in the room, naming, 80–81
  GMOOT, dealing with, 82
  LDC ("Listen, Decide,
    Communicate"), 78–80
  praise, sharing, 82–83
  repeatedly and consistently sharing the
    story, 76–78
  statistics on, 75–76
War cabinet bulldozer, 81–82
Whedon, Joss, 15
Which?, 11, 180
Wins, small and quick, 88–89
Win–wins, 29

Work Only with the Best (Power #3),
    57–62
  case study (Apple), 57–58
  case study (Asian beverage firm),
    58–59
  central question, 57
  conferences and, 61
  contribution to impact and success, 7t,
    59, 59t
  critical questions to answer, 61
  expense and, 60
  looking for success, 60
  talking to new partners, 61–62
Wozniak, Steve, 57

You Go First (movement-building)
    (Power #6), 85–91
  case study ("Greg," telecom company),
    86–87
  case study (chewing gum maker),
    88–89
  case study (Henkel Syoss), 87
  case study (Softbank), 89
  central question, 85
  contribution to impact and success, 7t,
    85, 86f
  critical questions to answer, 90
  the front line, 89
  language of customers and business,
    89–90
  quick small wins, 88–89
  starting a movement, 87–88
  tangible results and, 85
YouTube, 44

ABOUT THE AUTHORS

Thomas Barta (www.thomasbarta.com) is a former McKinsey partner and senior marketer. He speaks and writes to marketers on raising and achieving their growth aspirations. Thomas has consulted and marketed for over twenty years, in fourteen industries, in forty-five countries. He does extensive leadership research and, each year, gives more than forty keynotes and seminars for companies, industry associations, and universities around the globe. His clients include many of the world's most prominent companies, including over two dozen from the Fortune 500.

After a fast-track marketing career at Kimberly-Clark (Kleenex), Thomas joined McKinsey to help CEOs deliver profitable growth in a bigger way. As a dean of the firm's highest-rated internal program, he trained over a thousand McKinsey leaders on driving change without authority. He also shaped, for several years, McKinsey's highly successful global client relationship strategy efforts. For the CMO Fellowship Programme (a joint venture between McKinsey and the Marketing Academy to prepare CMOs for a CEO role), Thomas serves as its longstanding leadership dean.

Thomas holds a master's in business from Cologne University (OAS), an MBA from London Business School, and a master's in clinical organizational psychology from INSEAD Business School (France and Singapore).

Thomas lives in Cologne, Germany.
www.thomasbarta.com

Patrick Barwise (www.patrickbarwise.com) is emeritus professor of management and marketing at London Business School. He joined LBS in 1976 after an early career at IBM and has published widely on management, marketing, and media. His book, *Simply Better: Winning and Keeping Customers by Delivering What Matters Most,* coauthored with Seán Meehan (IMD, Lausanne), won the American Marketing Association's 2005 Berry-AMA Book Prize and has been translated into seven other languages. Their second book, *Beyond the Familiar: Long-Term Growth through Customer Focus and Innovation,* was published in 2011. Patrick is also former chairman of Which?, the UK's leading consumer organization and is an experienced expert witness in international commercial, tax, and competition cases. He has been involved in two successful business start-ups: online market research company Research Now (sold to e-Rewards in 2009) and online brand community specialist Verve (www.patrickbarwise.com).

■ ■ ■

www.marketingleader.org